Creating Logos with Illustrator

Creating Logos with Illustrator
By Peter Bone
Published by Designtuitive
www.designtuitive.com
©2017 Peter Bone. All rights reserved.
ISBN: 978-1-908510-39-6
Version 2.0 April 2017

I0093270

Notice of Liability
The information in this book is distributed on as "As
Is" basis without warranty. Whilst every precaution
has been taken in the preparation of the book,
neither the author nor the publisher shall have neither
liability nor responsibility with respect to any loss or
damages caused or alleged to be caused directly or
indirectly by the information contained within it.

Notice of Trademarks
Adobe, Illustrator, Indesign and Photoshop are trademarks
of Adobe Systems, Inc. QuarkXpress is the trademark of
Quark, Inc. Pantone is the trademark of Pantone, Inc.

Designtuitive.com
Create it yourself

If Hot Numbers in Cambridge didn't exist, neither would this book.

Thanks to everybody whose encouragement, help, support
and advice has helped Designtuitive continue and grow.
Special mentions are due for Caroline Bone, Ellie Doney,
Rob Francis, Chantal Freeman, Paul Northup, Paolo Pedretti,
Mark Rigby, Peter Rosenberg, Julia Ruxton, Sue Tomlin and Jo Wroe.
Thanks too to all our readers, viewers, followers, subscribers...
...we couldn't have done it without you.

CONTENTS

ABOUT THIS BOOK

I know both from my own experience and from having taught hundreds of designers that Illustrator has a reputation for being difficult. But I also know what a wonderful creative tool it can be once you start to feel confident. I have written this book in an attempt to get you to that point as quickly and directly as possible.

My hope is that whether you've just started using Illustrator or whether you've been struggling with it for years, that you'll learn a great deal of useful things here, and quickly. In particular I hope that you discover how, dare I say it, *easy* it can be to quickly create logos that can both look good, and are created with a degree of precision and accuracy. It's largely about knowing which of the large array of Illustrator's tools and features to use, how to use them, and in what combination. As you work through this book the skills you learn should build upon each other, and the process of creating things should become more and more intuitive: quick, easy, almost second nature.

By the time you've finished this book, as well as having created nearly fifty logos of different sorts, you'll have discovered some of the key skills used to create a whole variety of things in Illustrator. To keep things simple I've deliberately focused on a relatively small number of Illustrator's features. And in an attempt to mirror the creative constraints of a typical design job, I've restricted the elements used to either circles, triangles, rounded rectangles or typefaces. I've also limited the colours used to just black and white, which is partly to further stretch my and your creativity, but also by the belief that if a logo doesn't look good in black and white it's unlikely to look good in colour.

These are not true logos in that they have no company name attached (although the Yin / Yang symbol is of course something you'll have seen before) – but the skills and processes used in creating them are nonetheless the same. I have deliberately avoided copying actual company logos, but if I have inadvertently recreated yours, please accept my apologies. In describing the creation of these logos I've been very specific in an attempt to convey the process as clearly as possible. So please feel free to use different colours, different sizes, different options. In other words use this as a springboard to learn as much as you can and to stretch yourself creatively as much as you can.

HOW TO USE THIS BOOK

1. This book is designed to be read one section at a time. So whether you choose to start with the circles, triangles or type, you'll get the most by sticking with that section before you move onto another, as it's written with the assumption that as you progress through it, you are already familiar with the subjects covered earlier.

2. I've made two assumptions about you: firstly that your main interest is in creating things *with* Illustrator rather than merely acquiring knowledge *about* it. And secondly that you'll want to start creating logos immediately. If that's the case, simply continue to the next page where the exercises begin. I have, however, included some useful information about things like setting up workspaces and documents, and which file types and colour modes to use. These can be found in the *Brief Technical Notes* section that follows the logos, and can be read before or after you've created the logos, or not at all.

3. The steps for you to follow are listed in numbered paragraphs (like this).

4. When you need to select a tool or choose a menu command or press a button – in other words do something – it's written in **Bold**. It'll be written in ***Bold Italic*** if it's a feature you've not previously encountered in that section.

5. When you need to type in values, measurements or choose something from a pop-up menu, the value will be written in *Italic* as well as the area where you'll need to type it into. Some terms are also emphasised using italics.

6. The vast majority of the logos can be created with any Creative Cloud (CC) or Creative Suite (CS) version of Illustrator. Where a specific version is required it will be mentioned at the start. Specific approaches you might use if you're using Illustrator CC 2017 can be found on page 140.

7. The screenshots in the book are taken from the Mac version of Illustrator CC (18.1.1), using the default *Essentials* workspace (for more information on workspaces, see the start of the *Brief Technical Notes* section). Some small elements have been recreated to make them easier to see.

8. The only difference PC users need to be aware of is the use of the Command key, which on the PC is replaced with the Ctrl key. So for example, instead of the **Command+D** shortcut, type **Ctrl+D** instead.

Creating
Logos
from Circles

◉ LOGO 1

YOU DON'T NEED TO DO ANYTHING TO A CIRCLE TO MAKE IT LOOK GOOD, BECAUSE IT ALREADY DOES. ALL YOU'LL DO IN THIS FIRST LOGO IS SIMPLY CREATE TWO ADDITIONAL CIRCLES, ONE INSIDE THE OTHER.

1. From the **File menu** choose **New** to create a new document. In the dialogue box that appears, click on *Print* and press the **Create button.** You'll create all your logos in this document*. As this is by default *Letter* size, it's larger than the logos you'll create. So shortly you'll learn how to zoom in, out and around the page to see what you'll be looking at.

2. In the **Tools Panel** click on the **Rectangle Tool** and keep the mouse button held down until the other tools appear from beneath it.

3. Choose the **Ellipse Tool** and click once on the page. In the dialogue box that appears, type *20mm* for both the *Width* and the *Height* and press the **OK button.** You now have a circle of exactly 20Millimeters diameter. If you don't see mm in the dialogue box, either type in "mm" after the numbers or choose **Illustrator>Preferences>Units** (Mac) or **Edit>Preferences>Units** (PC) to edit Illustrator's preferences.

4. Before you go any further it might be useful to have a closer view of what you're doing. To see your work larger on the screen, hold down the **Command key** and press the **+ key** to zoom in. If you've zoomed in and you want to change which part of the screen you're looking at, drag either of the **Scroll Bars** located at the bottom and right edges of your document**.

5. Look at the diagram at the foot of the opposite page, showing the steps needed to create the logo. Your circle probably looks like the first one: white with a thin black line around the edge. Illustrator's language for this would be a white *fill* and a black *stroke*.

6. To change it to look like the second one in the step diagram firstly locate the **Fill button** (highlighted in diagram 6) that's found towards the bottom of the **Tools Panel** and click on it – this enables you to change the fill colour. »

---

* *There are a couple of alternative approaches you could take instead of creating one large document. These are discussed towards the end of the Brief Technical Notes section.*

** *To zoom back out again, hold down the* **Command key** *(Ctrl on PC) and press the* **– key.** *To see the whole screen, hold down the* **Command key** *and press the* **0 (zero) key.** *You can alternatively use the Zoom and Hand Tools (found immediately above the Fill and Stroke buttons) to do the same things.*

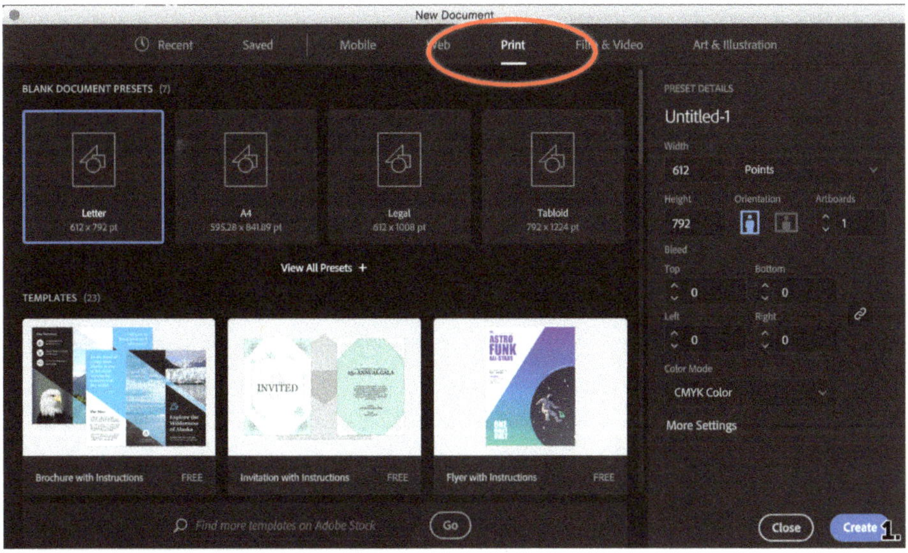
New Document
Recent
Saved
Mobile
Web
Print
Film & Video
Art & Illustration
BLANK DOCUMENT PRESETS (7)
Letter
612 x 792 pt
A4
595.28 x 841.89 pt
Legal
612 x 1008 pt
Tabloid
792 x 1224 pt
View All Presets +
TEMPLATES (23)
Brochure with Instructions
FREE
Invitation with Instructions
FREE
Flyer with Instructions
FREE
Find more templates on Adobe Stock
Go
PRESET DETAILS
Untitled-1
Width
612
Points
Height
Orientation
Artboards
792
1
Bleed
Top
Bottom
0
0
Left
Right
0
0
Color Mode
CMYK Color
More Settings
Close
Create
1.

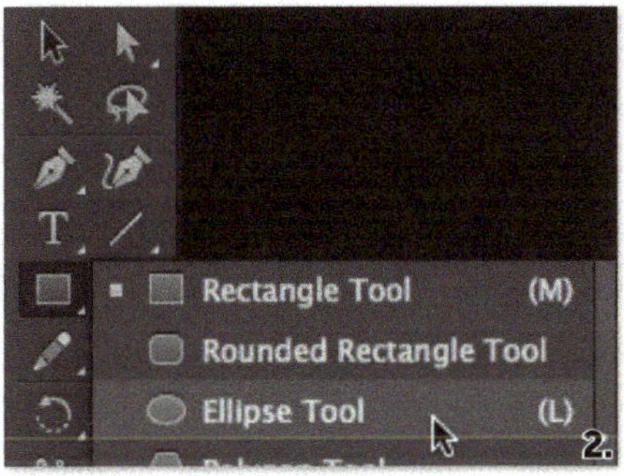
Rectangle Tool (M)
Rounded Rectangle Tool
Ellipse Tool (L)
2.

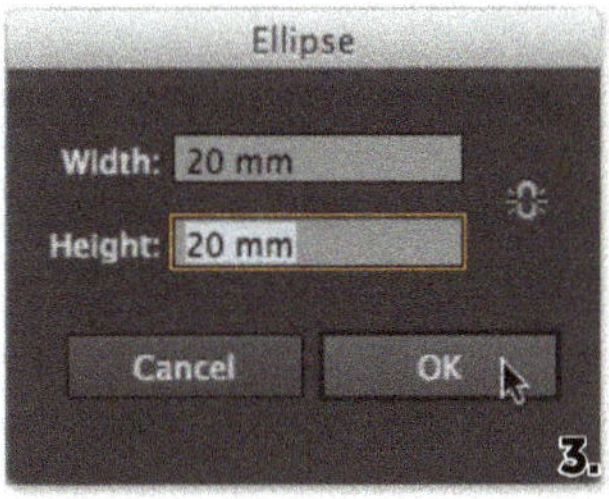
Ellipse
Width: 20 mm
Height: 20 mm
Cancel
OK
3.

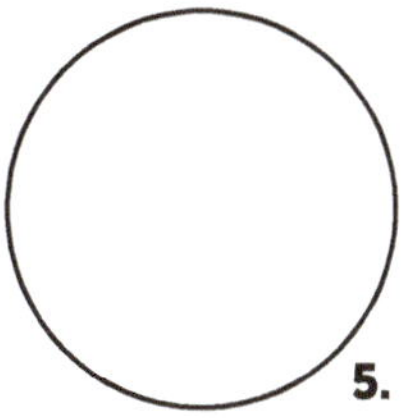

5.

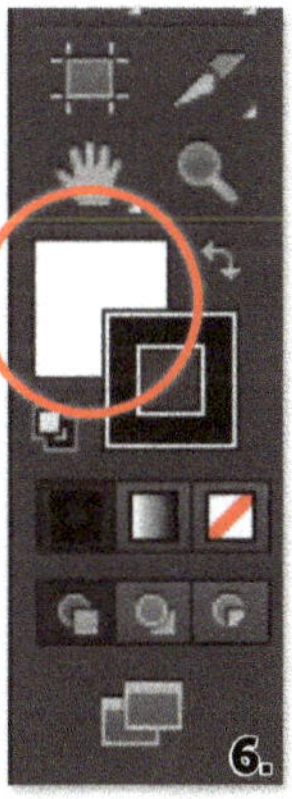
6.

7. To make the circle's fill black, firstly locate the button near the top right of your screen used to reveal the ***Swatches Panel,*** and click on it.

8. From the swatches that have appeared, click on the *black* one near the panel's top left.

9. In the **Tools Panel** click on the ***Stroke button**** (highlighted in diagram 9) that's next to the Fill button. Make the circle's stroke invisible by clicking on the leftmost *none* swatch in the top row of the **Swatches Panel.** In Illustrator version CC or CS6 you may have noticed the ***Color Panel*** appear – this is another way you can adjust the colour if you prefer.

10. In the **Tools Panel** double-click on the ***Scale Tool.*** In the dialogue box that appears type *60%* next to *Uniform.* Press ***Copy,*** and a new, smaller circle will appear exactly in the centre of the original**. As both circles are the same colour it's hard to see the new one, but if you look carefully you'll see the light blue *anchor points* that show the edge of the shape.

11. While the circle is still selected (as indicated by the *anchor points*) change its fill colour to *white* by clicking on the **Fill button** and choosing the *white* swatch from the **Swatches Panel.**

12. To finish the logo, double-click on the **Scale Tool** again to create a final circle (repeat Step *10* above), but this time create a copy with a *Uniform* Scale amount of *40%*. Change its *fill colour* to *black*.

---

* *What I have described as the Fill and Stroke buttons are not strictly buttons, but the areas on which you click to bring either the fill or stroke to the front, determining which will change when you apply a swatch.*

** *Illustrator automatically aligns copies around the centre when using the Scale Tool, which is generally very useful.*

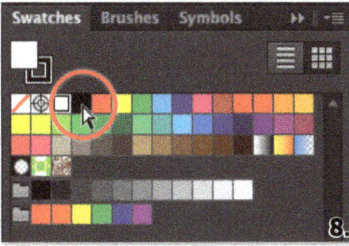

7.

8.

9.

10.

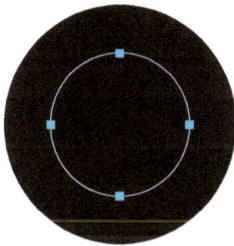

11.

12.

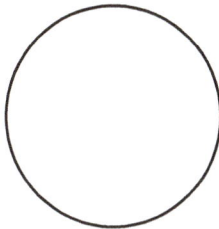

◯ LOGO 2

THE SECOND LOGO IS SIMILAR TO THE FIRST, BUT THIS TIME
WITH ONLY TWO CIRCLES INSTEAD OF THREE – AND OF COURSE
ONE OF THE CIRCLES HAS BEEN CHANGED INTO AN OVAL.

1. Continue working in the same document. Like other programs
    you'll have used, you can save files easily in Illustrator: choose **Save**
    from the **File menu** if you want to save your document (options
    will appear – stick with the default settings). Click on the page with
    the **Ellipse Tool** to create a circle of *20mm* diameter, as before*.

2. The fill and stroke colours on your circle should be the
    same as the last ones you used: a fill colour of *black* and
    a stroke colour of *none*. If they are not, change them by
    clicking on the **Fill** and **Stroke buttons** and applying the
    correct swatches from the **Swatches Panel,** as before.

3. Double-click on the **Scale Tool** to bring up the Scale dialogue
    box. Instead of applying a *Uniform Scale* to create a circular
    copy, apply a *Non-Uniform* Scale to create an oval. Press the
    Non-Uniform Scale radio button, enter *65%* for the *Horizontal*
    and *100%* for the *Vertical*. Toggle the **Preview checkbox** on
    and off to see the size that the new shape will be. If at this point
    you think it would look better if it was larger or smaller, adjust
    the numbers accordingly and toggle the **Preview checkbox** on
    and off again for a preview of the result. Once you've settled
    on the size and shape you want, press the **Copy button.**

4. To finish, click on the *white* swatch in the **Swatches
    Panel** to change the new oval's fill colour to *white*.

---

*   *Since Illustrator CS6, if you click the padlock at the right of the Ellipse dialogue box you
    only need to adjust the width or height and both values will change at once.*

Ellipse

Width: 20 mm
Height: 20 mm

Cancel   OK

1.

2.

Scale

Scale

○ Uniform: 40%
● Non–Uniform

Horizontal: 65%
Vertical: 100%

Options

☐ Scale Strokes & Effects
☑ Transform Objects   ☑ Transform Patterns

☐ Preview

Copy   Cancel   OK

3.

4.

LOGO 3 [CS4 onwards]

HERE YOU'LL SEE THE FIRST OF TWO METHODS YOU CAN USE TO ALIGN SHAPES QUICKLY AND ACCURATELY. THIS METHOD USES THE ENHANCED SMART GUIDES FOUND SINCE ILLUSTRATOR CS4.

1. Choose the **Ellipse Tool** and click once on the page. In the dialogue box that appears, type *10mm* for both the *Width* and the *Height* and press the **OK button.** Give the circle a fill colour of *black* and a stroke of *none.*

2. From the top left of the **Tools Panel** choose the ***Selection Tool.*** Click and drag to the right to move it a short way: this is what this tool does by default.

3. Drag again, but this time keep the ***Alt key*** held down at the same time, and notice the white arrow that appears. Release the mouse button whilst keeping the **Alt key** held down – and you will have created a copy of the shape instead of moving the original.

4. To align the circles accurately you'll use ***Smart Guides****. Firstly try and align the two circles vertically by slowly dragging one up or down until you see a thin line appear between them to indicate they are aligned. It is connected at both ends to an *x*, which indicates where they are aligned (at their centres). To align them horizontally move them closer together until they appear to snap together and another *x* appears at the point where they meet.

5. To finish the logo, drag the **Selection tool** with the **Alt key** to create two more copies of one of the circles, and align them all together using the visual clues provided by the smart guides, as before.

* *Smart Guides should be switched on by default; if they don't appear as you follow the instructions, choose* ***Smart Guides*** *from the* ***View menu*** *to switch them on.*

2.

3.

intersect

4.

5.

�֍ LOGO 3 [Any version of Illustrator]

BEFORE THE ENHANCED SMART GUIDES THAT ARRIVED WITH VERSION CS4 OF ILLUSTRATOR, A DIFFERENT METHOD WAS USED TO ALIGN SHAPES ACCURATELY. AS WELL AS BEING USEFUL FOR USERS WITH OLDER VERSIONS OF ILLUSTRATOR, IN SOME CIRCUMSTANCES IT CAN WORK BETTER THAN SMART GUIDES.

1. Follow the first three steps of the previous tutorial to create two circles, one to the right of the other.

2. In the *View menu* look at *Smart Guides* – there should be a small tick next to it, indicating that they are on. Choose **Smart Guides** to switch them off (you don't strictly need them to be off for this to work, but it's a lot easier to see what's happening with them off). Use exactly the same command to turn them on again later.

3. In the **View menu** choose *Hide Bounding Box**. The *Bounding Box* feature is on by default in Illustrator, and it enables you to re-size a shape with the Selection Tool. Whilst turning it off means you can no longer do that, it also means that you can more easily align shapes accurately with it.

4. Select the circle on the right with the **Selection Tool.** Notice the four small blue squares on the outermost points of the shape – the *anchor points* that define the shape. Hover your Selection Tool over the anchor point on the left of the shape and notice the small white square that appears, indicating that your cursor is accurately on this anchor point.

5. With the small square still showing, slowly drag the circle and try to align it accurately with the left circle. When your Selection Tool is perfectly aligned with the anchor point on the right of the original circle, it will turn white.

6. To finish, use the **Selection tool** with the **Alt key** to drag two more copies underneath the original circles. Align them all together by picking each one up by their topmost anchor points and aligning them with the anchor points on the bottom of the original circles.

*   Once you've finished this logo you'll have looked at two different approaches you can use to align objects. If you prefer this second method, you'll probably want to leave the Bounding Box and possibly the Smart Guides switched off. If you prefer the previous method you'll want to switch the Smart Guides back on (choose View>Smart Guides), and possibly turn the Bounding Box back on (choose View>Show Bounding Box).

1.

View Window Help

Rulers ▶
Show Bounding Box ⇧⌘B
Show Transparency Grid ⇧⌘D
Hide Text Threads ⇧⌘Y

Show Live Paint Gaps

Hide Gradient Annotator ⌥⌘G
Hide Corner Widget
Guides ▶
✓ Smart Guides ⌘U

Perspective Grid ▶

Show Grid ⌘'
Snap to Grid ⇧⌘'
✓ Snap to Point ⌥⌘'

2.

View Window Help

Hide Edges ⌘H
Hide Artboards ⇧⌘H
Show Print Tiling

Show Slices
Lock Slices

Hide Template ⇧⌘W

Rulers ▶
Hide Bounding Box ⇧⌘B
Show Transparency Grid ⇧⌘D
Hide Text Threads ⇧⌘Y

Show Live Paint Gaps

Hide Gradient Annotator ⌥⌘G
Hide Corner Widget
Guides

3.

4.

5.

6.

◯ LOGO 4 [CS5 onwards]

THIS LOGO AND THE NEXT TWO THAT FOLLOW IT WILL BE
CREATED USING STROKES AS OPPOSED TO FILLS. THIS ONE MAKES
USE OF THE SCISSORS TOOL TO CUT A CIRCLE IN TWO.

1. Using the **Ellipse Tool,** create a circle of *20mm* diameter.
   Apply a fill of *none* and a stroke of *black.*

2. In the **Tools Panel** click on the *Eraser Tool* and keep
   the mouse button held down until other tools appear
   from beneath it. Choose the *Scissors Tool.*

3. Ensure the circle you've just created is still selected (look to see the
   anchor points – if it's not selected, click on it with your **Selection
   Tool** and then change back to using the Scissors). With the **Scissors
   Tool** click once on the anchor point at the top of the shape (Smart
   Guides should help you click accurately on the anchor points).

4. Now click on the anchor point at the bottom of the shape. With those
   two "cuts" you have now effectively split the circle into two halves.

5. To see this more clearly, firstly choose the **Selection Tool** and click
   on an empty part of the page. Then click on each shape's stroke in
   turn to select them. As you can see there are two shapes, and they are
   perfectly aligned. Now all you need to do is add arrowheads on them.

6. Make sure both semicircles are selected: if only one is, hold
   down the *Shift key* and click on the other to select it too. Locate
   the *Stroke Panel* on the right of your screen (or alternatively
   choose *Stroke* from the *Window menu*). Then press the
   button on the top left of the panel to reveal more options.

7. At the bottom of the panel you'll now see two *pop-up menus* next to
   the word *Arrowheads.* On the right-hand pop-up menu choose *Arrow7.*

8. In the **Stroke Panel** change the stroke *Weight* to
   5pt and the *Scale* of the arrowheads to *20%.*

9. To finish*, select both semicircles and double-click on the
   Rotate Tool, enter *30* next to *Angle* and press **OK.**

* *It is common practice to "Outline" a logo created with strokes.
  You'll cover this when you create Logo 10.*

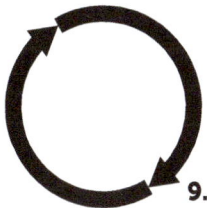

1.

2. Eraser Tool (Shift+E)
Scissors Tool (C)
Knife

Stroke Gradient Transparency
Weight: 1 pt

Stroke Gradient Transparency
Weight: 1 pt
Cap:

6.

Stroke Gradient Transparency
Weight: 5 pt
Cap:
Corner: Limit: 10 x
Align Stroke:
Dashed Line
dash gap dash gap dash gap
Arrowheads:
Scale: 100% 20%
Align:
Profile: Uniform

7.

8.

9.

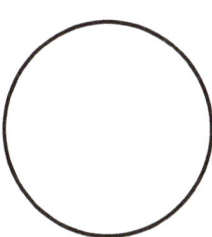
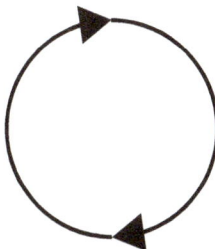
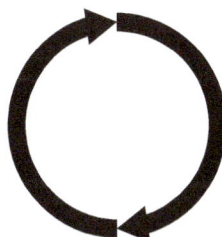

⊕ LOGO 5

YOU'VE ALREADY USED THE SCALE AND ROTATE TOOLS TO MAKE
SIMPLE TRANSFORMATIONS TO OBJECTS. FOR THE NEXT LOGO
YOU'LL TAKE THIS PROCESS FURTHER BY USING THE ROTATE
TOOL TO APPLY SOME MORE COMPLEX TRANSFORMATIONS.

1. Create a circle of *10mm* diameter. Give it a *black* stroke with
   a *Width* of *2pt* (in the **Stroke Panel**) and a fill of *none*.

2. Choose the **Rotate Tool.** You might recall that when you used the
   Scale Tool to create the first two logos, when you double-clicked
   with the tool it automatically re-sized the circle whilst keeping
   its centre in place. Illustrator's term for this place is the *Point of
   Origin* – and by default it's in the centre of a shape. The same thing
   applied when you double-clicked on the Rotate Tool when creating
   the previous logo – it rotated the semicircles around the centre.

3. However for this logo the aim is to create several copies of
   the circle that are rotated around its bottom anchor point.
   For this to happen you need to make Illustrator work in a
   way different to its default setting: hold down the **Alt key**
   as you click on the anchor point at the bottom of the circle
   (indicated with a square in diagram 3) with the **Rotate Tool.**

4. In the dialogue box that appears, enter *60* next to *Angle* and press
   the **Copy button.** This leaves the original circle in place, but creates
   a copy rotated at the desired angle, around the point you specified.

5. To complete the logo you'll need to repeat the above
   process another four times. A quicker way to do this
   is to repeatedly press the ***Command+D key****. This is a
   shortcut for ***Object>Transform>Transform Again,*** a
   command that repeats exactly the last *transformation*
   (a scale, move, copy etc) that Illustrator made.

*   **Ctrl+D** *if you're using a PC*

1.

2.

3.

Rotate

Rotate

Angle: 60°

Options: ✓ Transform Objects   Transform Patterns

Preview

Copy   Cancel   OK

4.

| Object | Type | Select | Effect | View | Window | Help |

Transform ► | Transform Again   ⌘D
Arrange ►

Group   ⌘G | Move...   ⇧⌘M
Ungroup   ⇧⌘G | Rotate...
Lock ► | Reflect...
Unlock All   ⌥⌘2 | Scale...
Hide ► | Shear...
Show All   ⌥⌘3

Expand... | Transform Each...   ⌥⇧⌘D
Reset Bounding Box

5.

LOGO 6 [CS5 onwards]

THIS LOGO IS VERY SIMILAR TO THE PREVIOUS ONE,
EXCEPT THAT IT MAKES USE OF A NEW FEATURE FOUND
SINCE CS5, THE WIDTH PROFILE OF A STROKE.

1. Create a circle of *10mm* diameter, with a *black* stroke and a fill of *none.*

2. In the **Stroke Panel,** change the stroke *Weight* to *4pt*
   and press the *Round Cap button,* which will make the
   ends rounded when the line becomes dashed.

3. Still in the Stroke Panel, click the ***Dashed Line checkbox*** to
   create a dashed line. Adjust the *dash* and *gap* values to create
   dash of *0pt* and a *gap* of *4pt.* Since Illustrator CS5 you can
   also press the button on the far right of the Dashed Line
   checkbox to automatically alter the dashed line to ensure
   the gaps are consistent across the whole of the stroke.

4. In the **Stroke Panel,** click on the **Pop-up menu** next to *Profile* and
   choose *Width Profile 1* (The one immediately under *Uniform*). This
   feature introduced in CS5 allows a stroke to follow a profile that
   controls its width. In this case the Width Profile makes the stroke
   thin at both ends and fatter in the middle. It can be especially
   useful when combined with a dashed line as you're doing here.

5. Now you'll use the **Rotate Tool** with the **Alt key** to create
   multiple copies around a specific point of origin. In the previous
   exercise I simply told you what angle of rotation to type in,
   but a handy alternative is to let Illustrator do the maths for
   you. As there are 360 degrees in a circle, once in the Rotate
   dialogue box, type *360/however many total circles you want*
   next to *Angle.* So in the finished example to create a total
   of 6 circles I typed *360/6* for *Angle,* then pressed **Copy.**

6. Try experimenting not only with the angle, but where you
   initially **Alt+click** with the **Rotate Tool:** it doesn't need to
   be on an anchor point – you can define the Point of Origin
   anywhere you like. Choose ***Undo*** from the ***Edit menu*** if
   you need to retrace your steps. To complete the logo use
   Command+D key or ***Object>Transform>Transform Again*** to
   create as many additional copies of the circle as you require. **26–27**

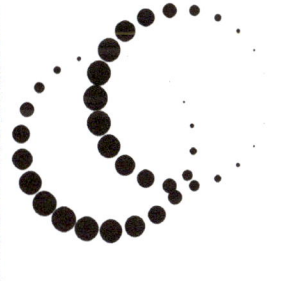

⊙ LOGO 7

TO COMPLETE THIS LOGO YOU'LL LOOK AT A USEFUL WAY TO CHECK HOW ACCURATELY OBJECTS ARE ALIGNED, AND TAKE A FIRST LOOK AT ILLUSTRATOR'S PATHFINDER PANEL.

1. Create a circle of *20mm* diameter, with a *black* fill and a stroke of *none.*

2. Create a circle of *10mm* diameter, with a fill of *white* and a stroke of *none.* Using either of the techniques you learned about when creating Logo 3, align the top of the white circle with the top of the black one. As the white circle is half the diameter of the black one, its bottom should sit exactly on the black circle's centre.

3. To check whether your shapes are properly aligned, deselect them and choose ***Outline*** from the **View menu.** This shows just the bare bones of the shapes, and can be useful when you want a clear picture of what you're doing*. As you can see, these circles have an "x" in their centre, so it's another way to check whether shapes are aligned or not. To change the view back, go back to the same place in the **View menu** and choose ***Preview.***

4. Use the **Rotate Tool** with the **Alt key** and **Transform Again** to create *3* copies of the white circle, all rotated *90°* around its bottom anchor point (or the central "x" if you're in Outline mode).

5. From the ***Window menu*** choose ***Pathfinder*** to show the Pathfinder Panel. Pathfinder commands are used to combine shapes in different ways, for example by adding them together or subtracting them from each other.

6. Using the **Selection Tool** in combination with the **Shift key,** select all of the white circles. Press the ***Unite button*** at the top left of the Pathfinder Panel. All of these separate shapes have now become one shape. Whilst the logo won't look any different, it's common practice to do this towards the end of the design process as it gives the logo a more finished feel.

7. Repeat the previous steps to create another arrangement of circles aligned in the centre, but this time using a circle of *5mm* diameter and a fill of *black.* Use **Pathfinder** again to unite the shapes. The finished logo, whilst appearing complex, is now only made of three shapes.

* *It's possible to work in Outline mode, but if you are, you can only select shapes by their edges or their centres.*

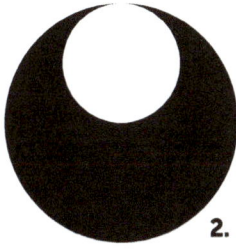

1.

2.

3.

4.

View   Window   Help

Outline   ⌘Y

Overprint Preview   ⌥⇧⌘Y
Pixel Preview   ⌥⌘Y

Proof Setup   ▶
Proof Colors

Window   Help

New Window
Document Info
Flattener Preview
Gradient   ⌘F9
Graphic Styles   ⇧F5
Image Trace
Info   ⌘F8
Layers   F7
Libraries
Links
Magic Wand
Navigator
Pathfinder   ⇧⌘F9
Pattern Options
Separations Preview
✓ Stroke   ⌘F10
SVG Interactivity
Swatches

5.

Transform   Align   **Pathfinder**

Shape Modes:

Expand

Pathfinders:

6.

7.

◆ LOGO 8

HERE YOU'LL LOOK AT A MORE COMPLEX PATHFINDER FEATURE.

1. Using the **Ellipse Tool** and the **Selection Tool,** create
    the same alignment of circles as you did in Logo 3
    (using your preferred approach to align them), but
    this time make the circles all *20mm* diameter.

2. Create another circle of *20mm* diameter but this time with
    a different coloured fill. Using **Smart Guides** and/or **Outline
    mode,** align it to the point in the centre of all the circles.

3. This new circle will define which elements are retained,
    and it will only work if it is in front of all the other circles.
    If it is not in front of the circles, select it and choose
    Arrange>Bring to Front from the **Object menu.**

4. If it is not already showing on your screen, choose *Pathfinder*
    from the *Window menu* to show the Pathfinder Panel.

5. Select all five of the circles* and press the *Crop button* on the
    bottom row of the **Pathfinder Panel.** This Pathfinder feature
    keeps only the areas of the selected shapes that overlap
    with the topmost object, and deletes everything else.

*   *It's often easier to select multiple objects with the Selection Tool using this method: begin with
    nothing selected, then click a little distance away from the objects, and keeping the mouse
    button down, drag the mouse. You'll notice a faint rectangle appear which indicates what will
    be selected. Make sure the rectangle either encloses or touches everything you want selected
    (but nothing that you don't), and let your mouse button go to select everything at once.*

1.

2.

intersect

Object Type Select Effect View Window Help

Transform ▶
Arrange ▶ | Bring to Front ⇧⌘]
| Bring Forward ⌘]
Group ⌘G | Send Backward ⌘[
Ungroup ⇧⌘G | Send to Back ⇧⌘[
Lock ▶
Unlock All ⌥⌘2 | Send to Current Layer

3.

Window Help

New Windows
Document Info
Flattener Preview
Gradient ⌘F9
Graphic Styles ⇧F5
Image Trace
Info ⌘F8
Layers F7
Libraries
Links
Magic Wand
Navigator
Pathfinder ⇧⌘F9
Pattern Options
Separations Preview
✓ Stroke ⌘F10
SVG Interactivity

4.

Transform Align **Pathfinder**

Shape Modes:

Expand

Pathfinders:

5.

✤ LOGO 9

TO CREATE THIS LOGO YOU'LL MAKE USE OF AN OLD
ILLUSTRATOR FEATURE – A GUIDE OBJECT – TO ASSIST
YOU IN MAKING A COMPLEX TRANSFORMATION.

1. Create a circle of *10mm* diameter, with a fill of *none* and a *black*
    stroke. In the **Stroke Panel** adjust the stroke *Width* to *3pt.*

2. Using the **Rotate Tool** in combination with the **Alt key,** rotate a
    copy of the shape *120°* around the circle's bottom anchor point.

3. Use the **Command+D key** or choose **Transform>Transform Again**
    from the **Object menu** to repeat once more and create a third shape.

4. Create another circle of *10mm* diameter and align its centre to the
    point of origin around which you just rotated the circles. From the
    View menu choose *Guides>Make Guides.* This turns an object into
    a guide, which means you can use it to align things, but it won't print.

5. Whether you can select a guide or not depends on whether
    Guides>Lock Guides is checked in the **View menu.** Since you are
    about to select all of the circles, you'll probably want to make sure
    your guides are locked so that you don't inadvertently select your
    guide as well. Look in the View menu, under Guides. If *Lock Guides*
    doesn't have a tick next to it, choose **Lock Guides** to lock them.

6. Select all three black circles and press the **Unite
    button** on the top left of the **Pathfinder Panel*.**

7. Select the **Rotate Tool.** Hold down the **Alt key** and carefully click
    on the "x" that marks the centre of the guide object. Rotate a copy
    of the shape *60°* around the centre of the guide object (as it's half
    the angle you previously used, it'll create a perfectly aligned copy).

8. To see what the final logo looks like without the guides,
    choose *Guides>Hide Guides* from the **View menu**.**

*   *It's possible that a small area might be left in the centre of the shapes. Should that happen, leave it for
     now, but once you've learned about the Group Selection tool in logo 11, come back and delete it.*

** *To turn the guides back on again, choose Guides>Show Guides from the View menu.*

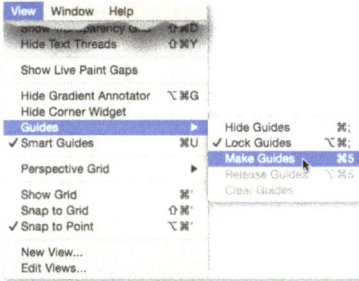

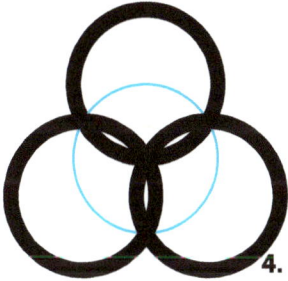

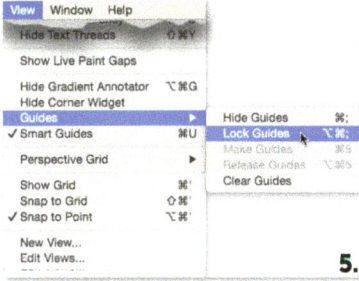

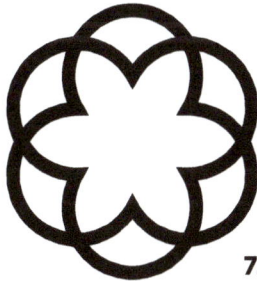

(8) LOGO 10

HERE YOU'LL LEARN HOW TO CONVERT SOMETHING THAT'S CREATED FROM A STROKE INTO A FILLED OBJECT, A PROCESS COMMONLY USED ONCE A LOGO'S DESIGN HAS BEEN FINALISED.

1. Using the **Ellipse Tool,** create one circle of *20mm* diameter and two circles of *10mm* diameter. Give all the circles a fill colour of *black* and a stroke of *none*.

2. To align the first circle go into *Outline mode* and align its top anchor point with the "x" that signifies the centre of the large circle.

3. Repeat the previous step with the other small circle, this time aligning its bottom anchor point with the centre of the larger circle.

4. Leave Outline mode by choosing **Preview** from the **View menu.** On both small circles change the fill colour to *none* and the stroke colour to *white*.

5. To finish the logo, in the ***Stroke Panel*** apply a *Width* of *10pt* to the white circles. This logo is now finished, but at this point it's common practice to convert the strokes to *outlines*. This re-creates the stroked objects as if they were filled objects. This finalises the process, making it impossible to accidentally make it thicker or thinner later (which might be just what you want once a logo's design is finished).

6. To convert the strokes to outlines, make sure they are selected and choose ***Path>Outline Stroke*** from the **Object menu***.

7. This is how the final logo will look, but if it was viewed on any colour other than white, the white would show against the background (see diagram 7). One way to prevent this is to make the white area transparent**.

8. Select all three shapes and press the ***Minus Front button*** on the top row of the **Pathfinder Panel.** The white shapes are cut away from the black, creating a transparent area that any background will show through.

* *It is good practice to save a copy of the logo before you convert the strokes to outlines, in case you want to go back and make any changes to it later.*

** *If the white colour was an integral part of the logo, of course you wouldn't want to make it transparent, but you would still want to get rid of the extra white area around the edge of the logo. The best way to do that would be to use Pathfinder's Divide button which you'll learn about in the next exercise.*

1.

2. center

3. intersect

4.

5.

| Object | Type | Select | Effect |

Rasterize...
Create Gradient Mesh...
Create Object Mosaic...
Create Trim Marks
Flatten Transparency...

Slice ▶

Path ▶   Join   ⌘J
Shape ▶   Average...   ⌥⌘J
Pattern ▶   Outline Stroke
Blend ▶   Offset Path...   6.
Envelope Distort ▶
Perspective

7.   8.

☯ LOGO 11

WHILST THIS LOGO MIGHT LOOK VERY COMPLEX, IT IS MUCH MORE SIMPLE TO CREATE THAN IT MAY FIRST APPEAR. IT IS MERELY A SERIES OF OVERLAPPED CIRCLES, SOME OF WHICH ARE JOINED TOGETHER.

1. Repeat the first three steps of the previous tutorial to create three perfectly aligned circles. Give them all a *white* fill and a stroke of *black*.

2. Create two circles of *2mm* diameter, giving them the same fill and stroke as the other circles. In the **View menu** choose **Outline,** and using **Smart Guides** align the centres of the smallest circles to the centres of the medium ones. To leave Outline mode, choose **Preview** from the **View menu.**

3. Select all the circles except the two smallest ones, and press the *Divide button* on the bottom left of the **Pathfinder Panel***. This divides the large circle into two pieces, one on the left and one on the right. Whilst the logo might not look very different yet, at every point where the shapes intersected, they have been divided.

4. To create the final logo you will need to select individual shapes which you will then combine. But if you try to do this using the **Selection Tool** you will find that when you click on any one shape you will select them all. This is because when you perform certain tasks (including Pathfinder commands) Illustrator creates a *Group* – and the Selection Tool always selects whole groups. So to select objects inside the group you will need to use the *Group Selection Tool* instead. In the **Tools Panel** press down on the **Direct Selection Tool** and when the *Group Selection Tool* appears, select it.

5. Using the **Group Selection Tool,** click on an empty part of the page to deselect everything. Then select both the top (medium sized) circle and the shape on the left, and press the *Unite button* on the top left of the **Pathfinder Panel.** Give this new shape a *black* fill.

6. Repeat the previous step to combine the bottom and right shapes, retaining the *white* fill and adjusting the stroke weight if you want to.

7. To finish, select the lower small circle and change its fill to *black* and its stroke to *none*.

* You could alternatively have used the Shape Builder Tool here – you'll use it in the next logo.   **36–37**

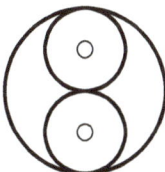

❀ LOGO 12

TO CREATE THE FINAL LOGO YOU'LL LOOK AT AN ALTERNATIVE
METHOD YOU CAN USE TO COMBINE COMPLEX SHAPES
IN DIFFERENT WAYS – THE SHAPE BUILDER TOOL.

1. Follow the first step in the previous logo exercise to
    create three perfectly aligned circles. For now, give all
    the circles a fill of *white* and a stroke of *black*.

2. With the **Selection Tool,** select all of the shapes. If you
    have Illustrator CS5 or later*, choose the ***Shape Builder
    Tool*** from the Tools Panel. This is generally a much more
    intuitive way to divide shapes up than using Pathfinder.

3. Starting to the left of the shapes, drag the **Shape Builder Tool**
    diagonally down through the large circle and onto the small
    circle at the bottom of the shape. Notice the "+" sign and the red
    highlighting of both shapes, indicating that it will merge the two
    shapes. Let go of the mouse button and the shapes will be merged.

4. Starting now from the right of the shape, drag the **Shape
    Builder Tool** diagonally up through the other half of the shape,
    but this time whilst holding down the *Alt key.* Notice the "−"
    sign and the green highlighting of both shapes, indicating
    that it will delete the two shapes. Let go of the mouse button
    and the shapes will be deleted, leaving the final shape.

5. From the **Tools Panel** choose the **Selection Tool.**
    Change the *fill colour* to *black* and the *stroke* to *none*.

6. Using the **Rotate Tool** in combination with the *Alt key,* click above
    the top right of the shape (see the dot on diagram 6 for guidance
    on where to click) and rotate a copy *90°* around this origin. Use
    Transform Again to repeat twice more and finish the logo.

* *If you have a version prior to CS5 you can still create the logo: using* **Pathfinder's Divide button**
  divide the shapes up like you did in the last exercise, combine two of them using **Pathfinder's**
  Unite button *and delete the rest using the* **Group Selection Tool** *and the* ***Delete key.***

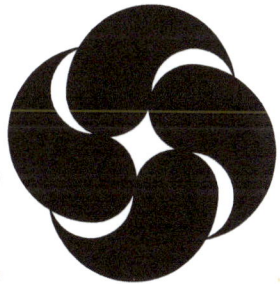

1.

2.

3.

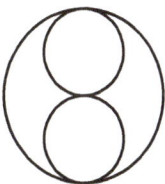

4.

5.

6.

Creating Logos from Triangles

△ LOGO 1

ARGUABLY THE BEST THING YOU CAN DO WITH A TRIANGLE IS LEAVE IT ALONE – IT IS QUITE BEAUTIFUL ENOUGH ON ITS OWN. ALL YOU'LL DO WITH THIS FIRST TRIANGLE IS TO MAKE SOME BASIC ADJUSTMENTS TO IT.

1. From the **File menu** choose **New** to create a new document. In the dialogue box that appears, choose *Print* from the options and press the **Create button.** You'll create all your logos in this document*. The default size is a lot bigger than the logos you'll create. So shortly you'll learn how to zoom in, out and around the page to see what you need to be looking at.

2. In the **Tools Panel** click on the **Rectangle Tool** and keep the mouse button held down until the other tools appear from beneath it. Choose the **Polygon Tool** and click once on the page. In the dialogue box that appears, type *20mm* for the *Radius, 3* for the number of *Sides* and press the **OK button.**

3. Before you go any further it might be useful to have a closer view of what you're doing. To see your work larger on the screen, hold down the **Command key** and press the **+ key** to zoom in. If you've zoomed in and you want to change which part of the screen you're looking at, keep the **Spacebar** held down as you click and drag with your mouse to reposition the screen**.

4. Look at the diagram at the foot of the opposite page, showing the steps needed to create the logo. Your triangle should look like the first one: white with a thin black line around the edge. Illustrator's language for this would be a white *fill* and a black *stroke*. To make the stroke thicker, firstly locate the **Stroke Panel** at the right of the screen, or choose **Stroke** from the **Window menu.** Then press the button at the very top left of the panel to reveal more options.

5. In the stroke panel, the **Weight** describes the thickness of the stroke – the default value is 1 point (1pt). Click on the popup menu to the right of the stroke weight to adjust it to around *20pt*. To finish, make the outer corners of the triangle rounded by clicking on the **Round Join button** (highlighted in diagram 5) in the **Stroke Panel.**

---

* *There are a couple of alternative approaches you could take instead of creating one large document. These are discussed towards the end of the Brief Technical Notes section.*

** *To zoom back out again, hold down the **Command key** (Ctrl on PC) and press the **– key.** To see the whole screen, hold down the **Command key** and press the **0 (zero) key.***

1.

2.

4.

5.

▲ LOGO 2

FOR THE SECOND LOGO YOU'LL LEARN ABOUT ANCHOR
POINTS, AND ADD AN EXTRA ANCHOR POINT TO CHANGE
THE SHAPE OF THE TRIANGLE. YOU'LL ALSO CHANGE
THE TRIANGLE'S FILL AND STROKE COLOURS.

1. Continue working in the same document. Like other programs
   you'll have used, you can save files easily in Illustrator: choose
   Save from the **File menu** if you want to save your document
   (options will appear – stick with the default settings).

2. Create another triangle by clicking once on the page with the **Polygon
   Tool.** The dialogue box that appears should contain the same numbers
   you typed in last time – giving you a triangle of 20mm radius. If
   not, enter *20* for *Radius* and *3* for *Sides* and press the **OK button.**

3. Notice the three small blue squares on each corner of the triangle.
   These are *anchor points,* and they define the edges of shapes in
   Illustrator. To change your triangle so that it looks like the final
   one in the step diagram at the foot of the opposite page you're
   going to add another anchor point to it and then amend it.

4. From the **Tools Panel** click and hold down on the *Pen Tool* until the
   other tools appear from beneath it. Choose the *Add Anchor Point
   Tool* and click carefully half way up the stroke on the right hand
   side of your triangle. If you don't click exactly in the centre of the
   stroke, a dialogue box will appear advising you how to use the tool.
   If this happens, press the **OK button** to dismiss it, and try again.

5. There are two types of anchor points: *corner* or *smooth.* Currently
   all your anchor points are corners because they have straight
   lines either side of them. To create the finished logo you'll change
   the anchor point you've just added to a smooth one, making the
   right hand side of your triangle curved. From the **Tools Panel** click
   and hold down on the *Add Anchor Point Tool* until the other
   tools appear from beneath it. Choose the *Anchor Point Tool.**

6. With the **Convert Anchor Point Tool** click on your
   anchor point and drag it diagonally to create a curved
   line. If you don't get the result you were looking for,
   choose *Undo* from the *Edit menu* and try again. »   **44–45**

---

* *Prior to version CC the Anchor Point Tool was known as the Convert Anchor Point Tool.*

2.

3.

4.

		Pen Tool	(P)
	+🖋	Add Anchor Point Tool	(+)
	−🖋	Delete Anchor Point Tool	(−)
	⌐	Anchor Point Tool	(Shift+C)

5.

6.

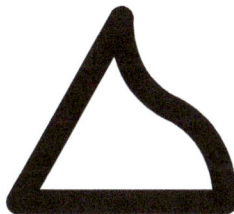

7. Look at the diagram at the foot of the opposite page, showing the steps needed to create the logo. Your triangle should currently look like the second one: it has a white *fill* and a black *stroke*. To change it to look like the final one in the step diagram firstly locate the **Fill button** (highlighted in diagram 7) that's found towards the bottom of the **Tools Panel** and click on it – this enables you to change the fill colour.

8. To make the triangle's fill black, firstly locate the button near the top right of your screen used to reveal the **Swatches Panel,** and click on it.

9. From the swatches that have appeared, click on the *black* one near the panel's top left.

10. In the **Tools Panel** click on the **Stroke button*** that's next to the Fill button.

11. Make the triangle's stroke invisible by clicking on the *none* swatch near the top left of the **Swatches Panel**.

12. To see what your logo really looks like you'll need to *deselect* it. Currently it is *selected,* meaning that Illustrator knows that you're working with it, and anything that you do will affect it. You can see it's selected because you can see the shape's blue anchor points. To deselect it, firstly choose the **Selection Tool** from the top of the **Tools Panel.** Then simply click on an empty part of the page.

* *What I have described as the Fill and Stroke buttons are not strictly buttons, but the areas on which you click to bring either the fill or stroke to the front, determining which will change when you apply a swatch.*

** *In Illustrator CC or CS6 you may have noticed the* **Color Panel** *appear – this is another way you can adjust the colour if you prefer.*

7.

8.

Swatches | Brushes | Symbols

9.

10.

Swatches | Brushes | Symbols

11.

12.

△ LOGO 3 [CS5 onwards]

IN CREATING THIS LOGO YOU'LL LEARN HOW TO SPLIT A TRIANGLE
INTO THREE DISTINCT PATHS, AND APPLY A WIDTH PROFILE TO
EACH STROKE, A FEATURE FOUND SINCE ILLUSTRATOR CS5.

1. Continue working in the same document and create another
    triangle by clicking once on the page with the **Polygon Tool.** The
    dialogue box that appears should contain the same numbers
    you typed in last time – giving you a triangle of 20mm radius. If
    not, enter *20* for *Radius* and *3* for *Sides* and press the **OK button.**
    Give the triangle a *black* **stroke** and a **fill** of *none,* using the Tools,
    Swatches and Stroke panels as you have done previously.

2. From the **Tools Panel** click and hold down on the *Eraser
    Tool* until the other tools appear from beneath it. Choose
    the *Scissors Tool* and use it to click carefully on each of your
    triangle's anchor points. This changes your triangle from being
    one *closed path* (one complete enclosed object) to three
    open paths. If you don't click precisely on the anchor points, a
    dialogue box may appear advising you how to use the tool. If
    this happens, press the **OK button** to dismiss it, and try again.

3. To proceed, all three paths will need to be selected. With
    the **Selection Tool,** click on one of the paths and hold
    down the *Shift key* and click on the others to select them
    too*. Sometimes it's not that easy to see when things are
    selected – but you should hopefully notice a thin blue line
    that connects the pair of anchor points for each path.

4. In the **Stroke Panel** give the paths a **weight** of *20pt.*

5. Finally, towards the bottom of the **Stroke Panel,** click
    on the **Pop-up menu** next to *Profile* and choose *Width
    Profile 1* (The one immediately under *Uniform*). This feature
    introduced in CS5 allows a stroke to follow a profile that
    controls its width. In this case the Width Profile makes the
    strokes thin at both ends and fatter in the middle.

---

* *It's often easier to select multiple objects with the Selection Tool using this method: begin with
nothing selected, then click a little distance away from the objects, and keeping the mouse button
down, drag the mouse. You'll notice a faint rectangle appear which indicates what will be selected.
Make sure the rectangle either encloses or touches everything you want selected (but nothing
that you don't), and let your mouse button go to select everything at once.*

1.

2.

- Eraser Tool (Shift+E)
- Scissors Tool (C)
- Knife

3.

4.

5.

Stroke Gradient Transparency

Weight: 20 pt

Cap:

Corner: Limit: 10 x

Align Stroke:

Dashed Line

dash gap dash gap dash gap

Arrowheads:

Scale: 100% 100%

Align:

Profile: Uniform

Uniform

⚠ LOGO 4 [CS5 onwards]

YOU'LL CREATE THIS LOGO IN A SIMILAR WAY TO THE LAST: IT'S A
TRIANGLE SPLIT INTO THREE OPEN PATHS, BUT THIS TIME EACH
FEATURES AN ARROWHEAD, A FEATURE FOUND SINCE ILLUSTRATOR CS5.

1. Continue working in the same document and create another
    triangle by clicking once on the page with the **Polygon Tool.** The
    dialogue box that appears should contain the same numbers
    you typed in last time – giving you a triangle of 20mm radius. If
    not, enter *20* for *Radius* and *3* for *Sides* and press the **OK button.**
    If the triangle doesn't have a *black* **stroke** and a **fill** of *none,*
    change them in the same way you did in the previous logo.

2. From the **Tools Panel** choose the **Scissors Tool.** Click carefully in
    the *middle* of each of your triangle's lines to split the triangle into
    three *open paths.* If you don't click exactly in the centre of the
    stroke, a dialogue box will appear advising you how to use the tool.
    If this happens, press the **OK button** to dismiss it, and try again.

3. To proceed, all three paths will need to be selected.
    Using the **Selection Tool** in combination with the **Shift
    key,** select all three paths as you did before.

4. Locate the **Stroke Panel** on the right of your screen. At the bottom
    of the panel you will see two *pop-up menus* next to the word
    Arrowheads. From the right-hand pop-up menu choose *Arrow7.*

5. To finish, in the **Stroke Panel** change the *Scale*
    of the arrowheads to *20%,* the stroke **Weight** to
    around *12pt* and the *Corner* to a *Round Join.*

1.

Eraser Tool (Shift+E)

✂ **Scissors Tool** (C)

🔪 **Knife**

2.

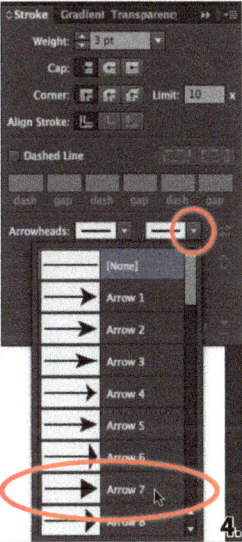

4.

Stroke | Gradient | Transparency

Weight: 12 pt

Cap:

Corner: Limit: 10 x

Align Stroke:

☐ Dashed Line

dash | gap | dash | gap | dash | gap

Arrowheads:

Scale: 100% | 20%

Align:

Profile: ——— Uniform

5.

△ **LOGO 5**

IN THE PROCESS OF CREATING THIS LOGO YOU'LL
LEARN HOW TO GIVE A PATH ROUNDED CAPS AND
HOW TO CONVERT A STROKE TO OUTLINES.

1. Repeat the first three steps of logo 3, to create a triangle that you've cut into three open paths.

2. Select all three paths and change the stroke **weight** to *40pt*.

3. Change the **fill** colour of all the paths to *none*.

4. Your triangle probably looks like the one in diagram two: each path is square at the end. To make each end rounded, press the ***Round Cap button*** in the **Stroke Panel.**

5. If you look at your triangle it consists simply of three open paths, each consisting of two anchor points – one at each end of each path. The paths look thick and rounded because each stroke has been given a large weight and rounded caps at each end. There are several occasions, however, when you'd want the shape to be defined by the actual anchor points and not by the settings of the stroke. This is what you'll need to do so that you can put a colour on the outside of the stroke. To do this, from the ***Object menu*** choose ***Path>Outline Stroke.***

6. If you look carefully at your triangle you can see that now it's made up of three rounded rectangle shapes, each with a fill of black and a stroke of none. A quick way to make the fills *none* and the strokes *black* is to press the ***Swap Fill and Stroke button*** near the bottom of the **Tools Panel.**

7. Increase the stroke **weight** to approximately *8pt* to finish the logo.

1.

2.

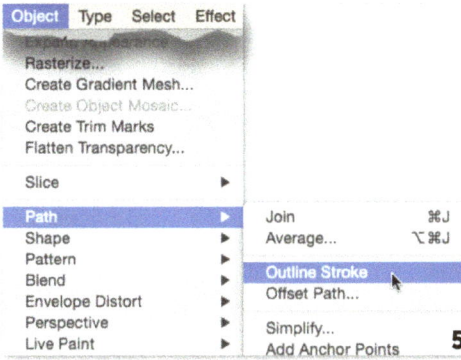

4.

5.

6.

7.

◤▽ LOGO 6 [CS4 onwards]

IN THE PROCESS OF CREATING THIS LOGO YOU'LL LEARN
TWO KEY ILLUSTRATOR SKILLS: HOW TO TRANSFORM A SHAPE,
AND HOW TO ACCURATELY ALIGN IT TO ANOTHER.

1. Continue working in the same document and create another triangle
    of the same size by clicking once on the page with the **Polygon
    Tool.** Change the stroke colour to *none* and the fill colour to *black.*

2. Double-click on the ***Rotate Tool.*** In the dialogue box
    that appears, enter *180* next to *Angle,* and press the
    Copy button. This leaves your original triangle alone, but
    creates a copy that's been rotated 180 degrees*.

3. Press the **Swap Fill and Stroke button** to give the new
    triangle a fill of *none* and a stroke of *black.*

4. Adjust the new triangle's stroke **weight** to about *12pt.* As the stroke
    weight increases, notice how half of it appears on the outside of the
    anchor points and half on the inside – this is Illustrator's default.

5. For this logo both triangles need to be the same size, so the stroke
    needs to be on the inside of the anchor points. To change this,
    in the **Stroke Panel** press the *Align stroke to Inside button.*

6. To align the triangles accurately you'll use ***Smart Guides**.*
    Change to the **Selection Tool** and try to align the triangles
    so that their edges meet exactly, as in the final step diagram
    at the foot of the opposite page. When you have got them
    accurately aligned they should appear to snap together.

*   *Illustrator automatically aligns copies around the centre when using
    the Rotate Tool, which is generally very useful.*

** *Smart Guides should be switched on by default; if they don't appear as you follow the
    instructions, choose **Smart Guides** from the **View menu** to switch them on.*

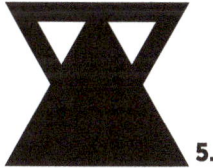

1.

2.

3.

4.

5.

6.

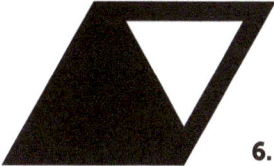

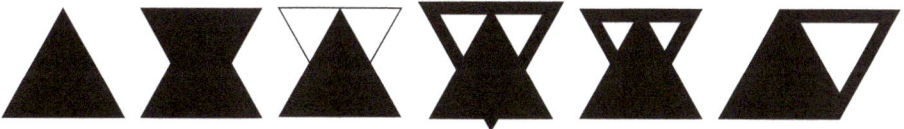

◣▽ LOGO 6 [Any version of Illustrator]

BEFORE THE ENHANCED SMART GUIDES THAT ARRIVED WITH
VERSION CS4 OF ILLUSTRATOR, A DIFFERENT METHOD WAS
USED TO ALIGN SHAPES ACCURATELY. AS WELL AS BEING USEFUL
FOR USERS WITH OLDER VERSIONS OF ILLUSTRATOR, IN SOME
CIRCUMSTANCES IT CAN WORK BETTER THAN SMART GUIDES.

1. Follow the first five steps of the previous tutorial to create
   the two different triangles, one on top of the other.

2. In the *View menu* look at *Smart Guides* – there should be a small
   tick next to it, indicating that they are on. Choose **Smart Guides** to
   switch them off (you don't strictly need them to be off for this to
   work, but it's a lot easier to see what's happening with them off).
   Use exactly the same command to turn them on again later.

3. In the **View menu** choose *Hide Bounding Box**. The *Bounding
   Box* feature is on by default in Illustrator, and it enables you
   to re-size a shape with the Selection Tool. Whilst turning
   it off means you can no longer do that, it also means that
   you can more easily align shapes accurately with it.

4. Select the newer triangle with the **Selection Tool.** Notice
   the three small blue squares on the outermost points of
   the shape – the *anchor points* that define the shape. Hover
   your Selection Tool over the anchor point on the bottom of
   the shape and notice the small white square that appears,
   indicating that your cursor is accurately on this anchor point.

5. With the small square still showing, slowly drag the triangle to the
   right and try to align it accurately with the right edge of the original
   triangle. When your Selection Tool is perfectly aligned with the anchor
   point on the base on the right of the original triangle, it will turn white.

* *Once you've finished this logo you'll have looked at two different approaches you can use to align objects.
If you prefer this second method, you'll probably want to leave the Bounding Box and possibly the Smart
Guides switched off. If you prefer the previous method you'll want to switch the Smart Guides back on (choose
View>Smart Guides), and possibly turn the Bounding Box back on (choose View>Show Bounding Box).*

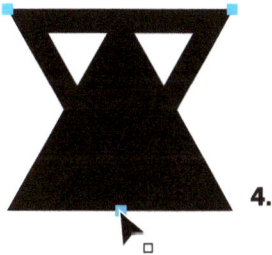

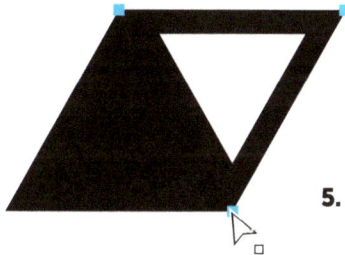

▲ LOGO 7

TO COMPLETE THIS LOGO YOU'LL SPLIT A TRIANGLE INTO TWO OPEN PATHS, THEN ADJUST THE CORNERS OF ONE OF THE PATHS TO CREATE A TRIANGLE WITH MIXED CORNERS.

1. Create a triangle of *20mm* radius, with a *black* stroke and a fill of *none*. In the **Stroke Panel** adjust the stroke's weight to *35pt**.

2. From the **Tools Panel** choose the **Scissors Tool.** Click once on the triangle's top anchor point and once on the anchor point on its right hand side*. This changes your triangle from being one *closed path* to two *open paths*.

3. Using your **Selection Tool,** click on an empty part of the page to deselect everything, then click carefully to select the open path on the right hand side of the shape. In the **Stroke Panel** change the cap from a *Butt Cap* to a *Round Cap* to round the two ends of the path.

4. Occasionally when you make adjustments in Illustrator it fails to redraw the screen accurately. Sometimes when you change corner options this can happen, and elements of the old corners appear to be left on the screen. If you zoom in or out using the **Command** and **+** or **−** keys, the screen will be redrawn and the old elements should disappear.

*   *If your triangle doesn't look like the one in diagram 1 (it has no gap in the middle), press the Align Stroke to Center button in the Stroke Panel.*

** *Smart guides are very helpful here – so if you've switched them off, you might find it helpful to have them on for this.*

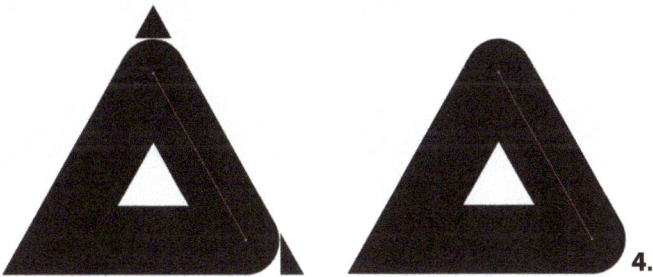

1.

2.

Stroke Gradient Transparency

Weight: 35 pt

Cap:

Corner: Limit: x

Align Stroke:

3.

4.

✳ LOGO 8

THIS LOGO IS MADE FROM AN ISOSCELES RIGHT TRIANGLE, WHICH YOU'LL CREATE BY AMENDING A RECTANGLE. YOU'LL ALSO LEARN HOW TO MAKE COMPLEX TRANSFORMATIONS WITH THE ROTATE TOOL.

1. In the **Tools Panel** click on the **Polygon Tool** and keep the mouse button held down until the other tools appear from beneath it. Choose the *Rectangle Tool* and click once on the page. In the dialogue box that appears, type *15mm* for both the *Width* and the *Height* and press the **OK button.**

2. Give the rectangle a **fill** of *black* and a *3pt* **stroke** of *white*.

3. In the **Tools Panel** click on the **Anchor Point Tool** and keep the mouse button held down until the other tools appear from beneath it. Choose the *Delete Anchor Point Tool* and click carefully on the rectangle's bottom left anchor point to remove it.

4. Look carefully at your triangle's anchor points and notice that one has a solid fill whilst the others are hollow. This means that only one anchor point of the triangle is selected. To continue you'll need to ensure that the *whole* triangle is selected. To do this, change to the **Selection Tool,** click once on an empty part of the screen to deselect everything, then click back somewhere in the middle of the triangle to select it.

5. Choose the **Rotate Tool.** You might recall that when you used it to create the sixth logo, when you double-clicked on it the triangle was automatically rotated around its centre point. For this logo the aim is to create several copies of the triangle that are rotated around the bottom right of the original. To do this you need to make Illustrator work in a way that's different to its default setting: hold down the *Alt key* as you click once on the anchor point at the bottom right of the triangle. In the dialogue box that appears, type *45* next to *Angle* and press the **Copy button.**

6. To complete the logo you'll need to repeat the above process another six times. A quicker way to do this is to repeatedly press the *Command+D** keys. This is a shortcut for *Object>Transform>Transform Again,* a command that repeats exactly the last transformation (such as a scale, move or copy) that Illustrator made.

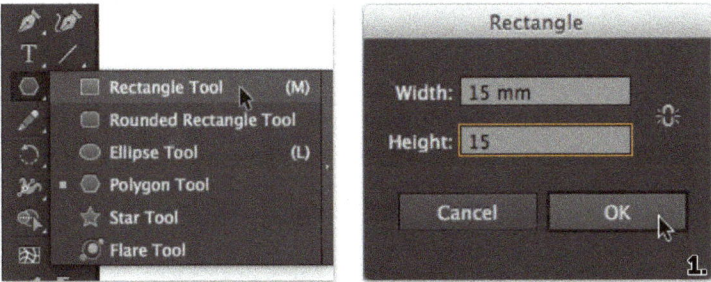

⬙ LOGO 9

IN THE CREATION OF THIS LOGO YOU'LL USE THE REFLECT TOOL, AND LEARN HOW AND WHY TO CREATE OUTLINES – A PROCESS COMMONLY USED AT THE END OF A LOGO'S CREATION.

1. To begin, repeat the first four steps of the previous logo. Change the triangle's **stroke** colour to *none*. Using the **Selection Tool,** hold down the **Alt key** and drag to create two copies of your triangle.

2. Using either of the alignment techniques you learned about when creating logo 6, align them together accurately so that they look like the triangles in diagram 2. Knowing what you already know, you could make copies of the triangles, rotate them and align them into place. Instead you'll use an alternative approach, and make use of another of Illustrator's transformation tools, the *Reflect Tool.*

3. Select all of the triangles. In the **Tools Panel** press on the **Rotate Tool** and keep the mouse button held down until the other tools appear from beneath it. Choose the **Reflect Tool.**

4. Double click on the **Reflect Tool** in the **Tools Panel.** In the dialogue box that appears, enter *-45* next to *Angle,* and press the **Copy button.** Like the rotate tool this creates a copy of the triangles, but this time they are a reflection instead of a rotation of the originals.

5. With the **Selection Tool** drag through all the triangles to select them and press the **Swap Fill and Stroke button** to make their fills *none* and their strokes *black*.

6. Increase the stroke **weights** to *4pt* and give the **corners** a *round join*.

7. This logo is now finished, but at this point it's common practice to convert the strokes to *outlines**. This re-creates the stroked objects as if they were filled objects. This finalises the process, making it impossible to accidentally make it thicker or thinner later** (which might be just what you want once a logo's design is finished). To convert the strokes to outlines choose **Path>Outline Stroke** from the **Object menu.**

*   All the preceding logos you have created using objects with strokes would normally be finalised by converting to outlines, as would those that you'll create from now on.

** It is good practice to save a copy of the logo before you convert the strokes to outlines, in case you want to go back and make any changes to it later.

1.

2.

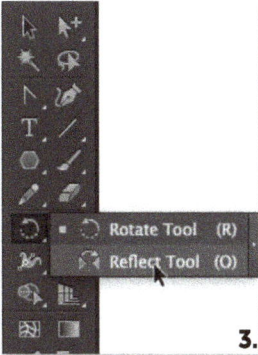

3.

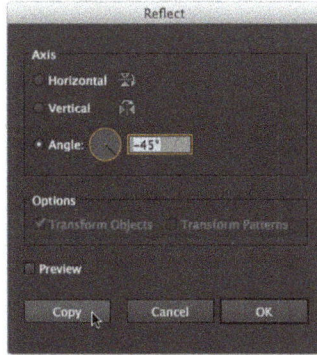

4.

5.

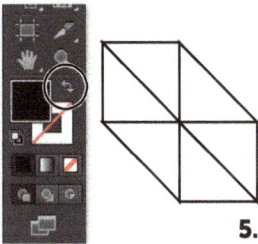

6.

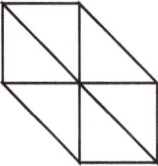

Object   Type   Select   Effect

Expand as outlines
Rasterize...
Create Gradient Mesh...
Create Object Mosaic...
Create Trim Marks
Flatten Transparency...

Slice   ▶

Path   ▶   Join   ⌘J
Shape   ▶   Average...   ⌥⌘J
Pattern   ▶   **Outline Stroke**
Blend   ▶   Offset Path...   **7.**
Envelope Distort   ▶

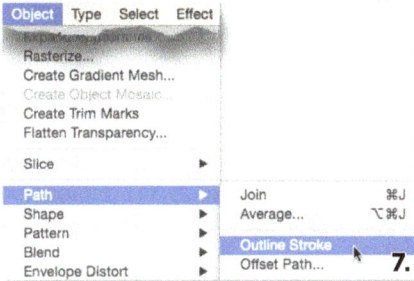

♣ LOGO 10

DURING THE CREATION OF THIS LOGO YOU'LL MAKE USE
OF ONE OF ILLUSTRATOR'S PATHFINDER FILTERS, AND GET A
DIFFERENT VIEW OF THINGS BY USING OUTLINE MODE.

1. To start, either recreate logo 5, or create a copy of it to work on.

2. Making sure all three shapes are selected, press the **Swap Fill and Stroke button** to make the fills *black* and the strokes *none*.

3. From the **Window menu** choose *Pathfinder* to show the **Pathfinder Panel.** Pathfinder commands are used to combine shapes in different ways, for example by adding them together or subtracting them from each other.

4. Making sure all the shapes are selected, press the *Divide button* on the bottom-left of the **Pathfinder Panel.** Whilst the logo might not look very different yet, at every point where the shapes intersected, they have been divided, as indicated in diagram 4.

5. To create the final logo you will need to delete the three shapes in the centre leaving just the three on the corners. If you try to do this using the **Selection Tool** you will find that when you click on any one shape you will select them all. This is because when you perform certain tasks (including Pathfinder commands) Illustrator creates a *Group* – and the Selection Tool always selects whole groups. So to select objects inside the group you will need to use the *Group Selection Tool* instead. In the **Tools Panel** press down on the **Direct Selection Tool** and when the *Group Selection Tool* appears, select it.

6. Click on a blank area of the page to deselect all the shapes. Then one at a time, select the three inner shapes and press the **Delete key** to delete them.

7. Choose *Outline** from the **View menu.** *Outline mode* shows just the bare bones of the shapes, and as you can see, shows there is a triangle left in the centre of the final shapes. Select this triangle by clicking on its edge, and delete it. As you drag the corner shapes in to align them you might notice some stray anchor points left behind. Drag around them with the **Group Selection Tool** to select them, and delete them too.

* *To change the view back, go back to the same place in the* **View** *menu and choose* **Preview.**

1.

2.

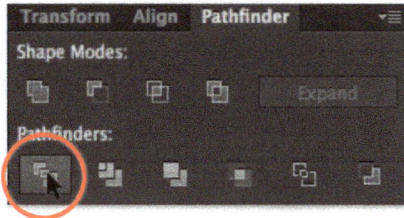

Window Help

New Window
Document Info
Flattener Preview
Gradient ⌘F9
Graphic Styles ⇧F5
Image Trace
Info ⌘F8
Layers F7
Libraries
Links
Magic Wand
Navigator
Pathfinder ⇧⌘F9
Pattern Options
Separations Preview
✓ Stroke ⌘F10
SVG Interactivity

3.

Transform Align **Pathfinder**

Shape Modes:

Expand

Pathfinders:

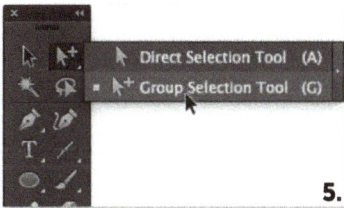

4.

Direct Selection Tool (A)
Group Selection Tool (G)

5.

6.

View Window Help

Outline ⌘Y

Overprint Preview ⌥⇧⌘Y
Pixel Preview ⌥⌘Y

Proof Setup ▶
Proof Colors

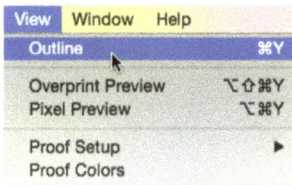

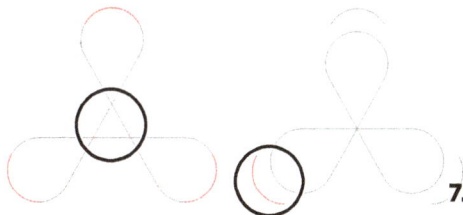

7.

✦ LOGO 11

DURING THE CREATION OF THIS LOGO YOU'LL LEARN
HOW ILLUSTRATOR CAN HELP YOU MAKE MATHEMATICAL
CALCULATIONS TO ASSIST IN COMPLEX TRANSFORMATIONS.

1. Use the Polygon Tool to create a triangle of *7mm*
radius, with a fill of *black* and a stroke of *none*.

2. In the **Tools Panel** click on the **Reflect Tool** and keep the mouse
button held down until the other tools appear from beneath it.
Choose the **Rotate Tool.** Double-click on it, and in the dialogue box
that appears, enter *180* next to *Angle,* and press the **Copy button.**

3. Using either of the alignment techniques you learned
about when creating logo 6, use the **Selection Tool**
to align them together so that their bases meet.

4. Select both triangles and return to the **Rotate Tool.** Hold down the
Alt key as you click on the anchor point at the bottom point of the
pair of triangles. In the previous exercises I have told you what angle
of rotation to type in, but a handy alternative is to let Illustrator do
the maths for you. As there are 360 degrees in a circle, once in
the Rotate dialogue box, type *360/however many total copies you
want* next to *Angle.* So in the finished example to create a total
of 6 pairs of triangles, type *360/6* for *Angle,* then press **Copy.**

5. To complete the transformations you'll need to repeat the
above process another four times, using the **Command+D**
shortcut for **Object>Transform>Transform Again.**

6. To complete the logo, select all of the triangles
and give them a *white 4pt* stroke.

7. Whilst the logo appears finished, the gaps that appear around
the triangles would only show if the logo is placed upon a
white background. To make the logo more flexible, a better
approach would be to delete all of the white areas so that there
is a real gap instead of a white stroke. This is something you'll
learn how to do when creating the next and final logo.

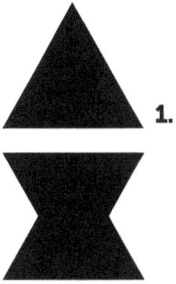

1.

2.

3.

4.

5.

6.

7.

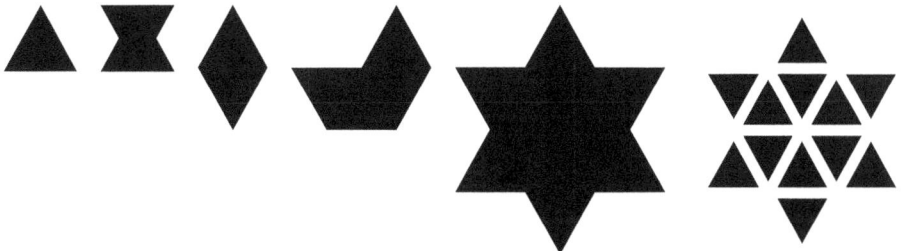

⊘ LOGO 12

FOR THE FINAL LOGO YOU'LL LEARN TO
CREATE A REAL GAP BETWEEN PATHS

1. Follow the first four steps of logo 8 to create an Isosceles
   Right triangle from a rectangle. Make sure the whole triangle is
   selected, and give it a **fill** of *black* and a *3pt grey* **mitred** *stroke*.

2. From the **Effect menu** choose **Stylize>Rounded corners.**
   In the dialogue box that appears, enter a *Radius* of *1mm*.
   This is an example of appearance, which changes the look
   of an object without changing its anchor points.

3. Using the technique you used in logo 11, use the **Rotate Tool** to create a
   total of eight triangles rotated around the triangle's bottom anchor point.

4. From the **View menu** choose **Outline.** In outline mode you can see
   that even though the triangles appear to have rounded corners, their
   original anchor points are unchanged. Stay in outline mode and align
   the triangles so that they look like those in diagram 4. Remember
   that you can only select objects by their edges in outline mode.

5. From the **View menu** choose **Preview.** In this mode you can see that
   whilst the shapes are aligned, you'll need to get rid of the grey strokes to
   create a gap between them. Whilst you could make them white as you
   did in the last logo, it is better to delete them. Firstly select all the triangles
   and outline their strokes (as you did in logo 9). Then using the **Group
   Selection Tool,** deselect everything, then click on a black triangle and
   delete it. Repeat for all the black triangles, then return to **Outline mode.**

6. Each remaining triangle is a *Compound Path:* the outer triangle
   defines the outside of the path and the inner one defines the
   inside. Using the **Group Selection Tool,** carefully select and
   delete each outer triangle until you're left with the final shapes.

7. To finish, select all the final shapes and give them each a *black* fill.

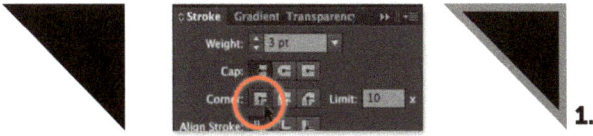

1.

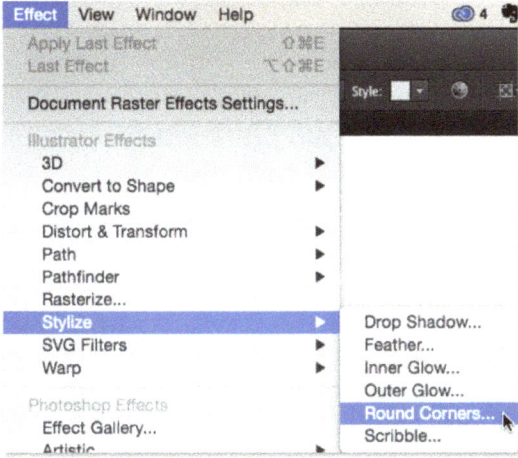

2.

3.

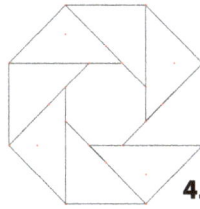

4.

5.

6.

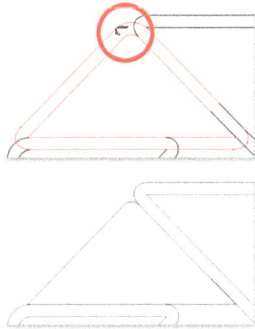

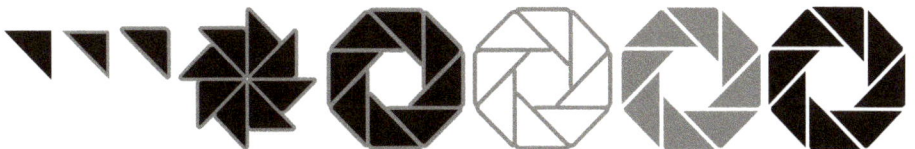

Creating Logos from Rounded Rectangles

✚ LOGO 1

IN CREATING THIS FIRST LOGO YOU'LL LEARN HOW
TO CREATE A ROUNDED RECTANGLE AND THEN
HOW TO MAKE A ROTATED COPY OF IT.

1. From the *File menu* choose *New* to create a new document. In
    the dialogue box that appears, choose *Print* from the options
    and press the *Create button.* You'll create all your logos in
    this document*. The default size is a lot bigger than the logos
    you'll create. So shortly you'll learn how to zoom in, out and
    around the page to see what you need to be looking at.

2. In the **Tools Panel** click on the *Rectangle Tool* and keep the mouse
    button held down until the other tools appear from beneath it.

3. Choose the *Rounded Rectangle Tool* and click once on the page.
    In the dialogue box that appears, type *7mm* for the *Width, 20mm* for
    the *Height, 4mm* for the *Corner Radius* and press the **OK button.**

4. Before you go any further it might be useful to have a closer view
    of what you're doing. To see your work larger on the screen,
    hold down the *Command key* and press the *+ key* to zoom in.
    If you've zoomed in and you want to change which part of the
    screen you're looking at, keep the *Spacebar* held down as you
    click and drag with your mouse to reposition the screen**.

5. Look at the diagram at the foot of the opposite page, showing
    the steps needed to create the logo. Your shape probably looks
    like the first one: white with a thin black line around the edge.
    Illustrator's language for this would be a white *fill* and a black *stroke*.

6. To change it to look like the second one in the step diagram
    firstly locate the *Fill button* (highlighted in diagram 6)
    that's found towards the bottom of the **Tools Panel** and
    click on it – this enables you to change the fill colour. »

*   *There are a couple of alternative approaches you could take instead of creating one large
    document. These are discussed towards the end of the Brief Technical Notes section.*

** *To zoom back out again, hold down the **Command key** (Ctrl on PC) and press the **– key.** To see the
    whole screen, hold down the **Command key** and press the **0 (zero) key.** You can alternatively use the
    Zoom and Hand Tools (found immediately above the Fill and Stroke buttons) to do the same things.*

7. To make the fill black, firstly locate the button near the top right of your screen used to reveal the **Swatches Panel,** and click on it.

8. From the swatches that have appeared, click on the *black* one near the panel's top left.

9. In the **Tools Panel** click on the **Stroke button** that's next to the Fill button*.

10. Make the shape's stroke invisible by clicking on the *none* swatch in the very top left of the **Swatches Panel.** In Illustrator CC or CS6 you may have noticed the **Color Panel** appear. This is another way you can adjust the colour if you prefer.

11. Double-click on the **Rotate Tool.**

12. In the dialogue box that appears type *90* next to *Angle* and press **Copy,** and a copy of your shape is rotated *90* degrees around its centre – creating the finished logo**.

* *What I have described as the Fill and Stroke buttons are not strictly buttons, but the areas on which you click to bring either the fill or stroke to the front, determining which will change when you apply a swatch.*

** *Illustrator automatically aligns copies around the centre when using the Rotate Tool, which is generally very useful.*

7.

8.

9.

10.

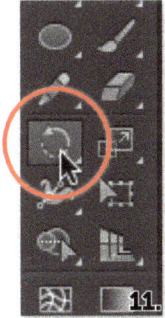

11.

Rotate

Rotate

Angle: 90°

Options: ✓ Transform Objects   Transform Patterns

✓ Preview

Copy   Cancel   OK

12.

❤ LOGO 2 [CS4 onwards]

HERE YOU'LL SEE THE FIRST OF TWO METHODS YOU CAN USE TO
ALIGN SHAPES QUICKLY AND ACCURATELY. THIS METHOD USES THE
ENHANCED SMART GUIDES FOUND SINCE ILLUSTRATOR CS4*.

1. Continue working in the same document. Like other programs
    you'll have used, you can save files easily in Illustrator: choose
    Save from the **File menu** if you want to save your document
    (options will appear – stick with the default settings).

2. To start creating this logo, either repeat the steps in the previous
    logo to get two aligned rounded rectangles or copy the previous
    logo. To do this, choose the *Selection Tool* from the top of the
    Tools Panel and click on the first shape to select it, then hold
    down the *Shift key* as you click on the other shape to select that
    as well. From the *Edit menu* choose *Copy* and then *Paste.*

3. To align the shapes accurately you'll use *Smart Guides**.* Firstly try
    and align the two shapes horizontally by dragging the wide shape
    slowly to the right. When the left edge of both shapes touch you
    should see a green line appear at the point they meet, along with
    the word "intersect". This indicates the two objects are aligned.

4. To align the shapes vertically move the wide shape slowly
    down until they appear to snap together and another
    line appears at the point at which they meet.

5. Both shapes now need to be rotated, and to do that
    they both need to be selected. To select both the
    shapes, follow the instructions in step 2, above.

6. To complete the logo double-click on the **Rotate Tool.** In the dialogue
    box that appears type *45* next to *Angle* and press the **OK button.**

* *If you have a version prior to CS4 or want to know a different way of aligning shapes, then follow the next tutorial.*

** *Smart Guides should be switched on by default; if they don't appear as you follow the
    instructions, choose **Smart Guides** from the **View Menu** to switch them on.*

2.

intersect

3.

intersect

4.

6.

❤ LOGO 2 [Any version of Illustrator]

BEFORE ILLUSTRATOR CS4'S ENHANCED SMART GUIDES
ARRIVED, SHAPES WERE ALIGNED USING A DIFFERENT METHOD.
AS WELL AS BEING ESSENTIAL FOR USERS WITH OLDER
VERSIONS OF ILLUSTRATOR, I FIND THAT THIS APPROACH
OFTEN WORKS BETTER THAN USING SMART GUIDES.

1. To start creating this logo, repeat the first step of the previous logo to get two aligned rounded rectangles. Change the **Fill colour** of the tall rounded rectangle so that it's easier to see what's happening as you align the shapes.

2. In the *View menu* look at *Smart Guides* – there should be a small tick next to it, indicating that they are on. Choose **Smart Guides** to switch them off (you don't strictly need them to be off for this to work, but it's a lot easier to see what's happening with them off). Use exactly the same command to turn them on again later.

3. In the **View menu** choose *Hide Bounding Box.* This feature is on by default in Illustrator, and it enables you to re-size a shape with the Selection Tool. Whilst turning it off means you can no longer do that, it also means that you can more easily align shapes accurately with it*.

4. Select the wide rectangle with the **Selection Tool.** Notice the six small blue squares on the outermost points of the shape – these *Anchor Points* define the shape of objects in Illustrator. Hover your **Selection Tool** over the anchor point on the left of the shape and notice the small white square that appears, indicating that your cursor is on top of this anchor point.

5. With the small square still showing, drag the shape and try to align it accurately with the bottom left anchor point of the other shape. When your Selection Tool is perfectly aligned with the anchor point, it will turn white, meaning the shapes are accurately aligned. If you don't get it right first time, choose *Undo* from the **Edit menu** and try again.

6. To finish, make the fill colour of both shapes the same, select both shapes and double-click on the **Rotate Tool.** In the dialogue box that appears type *45* next to *Angle* and press the **OK** button.

---

* *Once you've finished this logo you'll have looked at two different approaches you can use to align objects. If you prefer this second method, you'll probably want to leave the Bounding Box and possibly the Smart Guides switched off. If you prefer the previous method you'll want to switch the Smart Guides back on (choose View>Smart Guides), and possibly turn the Bounding Box back on (choose View>Show Bounding Box).* **78–79**

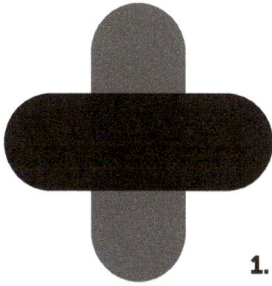

1.

View Window Help

Rulers ▶
Show Bounding Box ⇧⌘B
Show Transparency Grid ⇧⌘D
Hide Text Threads ⇧⌘Y

Show Live Paint Gaps

Hide Gradient Annotator ⌥⌘G
Hide Corner Widget
Guides ▶
✓ Smart Guides ⌘U

2.

View Window Help

Hide Edges ⌘H
Hide Artboards ⇧⌘H
Show Print Tiling

Show Slices
Lock Slices

Hide Template ⇧⌘W

Rulers ▶
Hide Bounding Box ⇧⌘B
Show Transparency Grid ⇧⌘D
Hide Text Threads ⇧⌘Y

3.

4.

5.

Rotate

Rotate

Angle: 45°

Options: ✓ Transform Objects   Transform Patterns

☑ Preview

Copy   Cancel   OK

6.

→ LOGO 3

HERE YOU'LL COMBINE WHAT YOU CREATED IN THE
PREVIOUS LOGO AND ADD A THIRD, LONGER ROUNDED
RECTANGLE TO CREATE AN ARROW SHAPE.

1. Follow the steps of either of the two previous
   tutorials to re-create the previous logo.

2. Make sure that both shapes are selected and double-
   click with the **Rotate Tool** to rotate it *90* degrees.

3. Make sure that both shapes are still selected, and from the
   Object menu choose *Group.* Grouping the shapes means
   that even though they are still two separate objects, when you
   select them they behave as one, which will be useful later.

4. Choose the **Rounded Rectangle Tool** and click on
   the page. This time enter *30mm* for the *Width, 7mm*
   for the *Height, 4mm* for the *Corner Radius.*

5. Select both the new wide rectangle and the group by using the
   Selection Tool in combination with the **Shift key** as before*.

6. To align the shapes firstly locate the *Align
   Panel.* by choosing *Window>Align**.*

7. To align them vertically click on the *Vertically Align Center
   button* (the second from right button in the top row). To align
   them horizontally click the *Horizontally Align Right button*
   (the third button from the left in the top row). It's possible that
   your shapes will seem to disappear when you press the align
   buttons (because they have moved). If so, zoom out to get a view
   of the whole page and you should be able to locate them.

* *It's often easier to select multiple objects with the Selection Tool using this method: begin with
  nothing selected, then click a little distance away from the objects, and keeping the mouse
  button down, drag the mouse. You'll notice a faint rectangle appear which indicates what will
  be selected. Make sure the rectangle either encloses or touches everything you want selected
  (but nothing that you don't), and let your mouse button go to select everything at once.*

** *In recent versions of Illustrator the align buttons also appear automatically in the Control
   Panel at the top of the screen when more than one object is selected.*

1.

Object Type Select Effect
Transform ▶
Arrange ▶
Group ⌘G
Ungroup ⇧⌘G
Lock ▶
Unlock All ⌥⌘2
Hide ▶
Show All ⌥⌘3

3.

Rounded Rectangle
Width: 30 mm
Height: 7 mm
Corner Radius: 4 mm
Cancel   OK

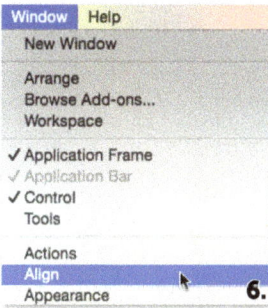

4.

Window Help
New Window

Arrange
Browse Add-ons...
Workspace

✓ Application Frame
✓ Application Bar
✓ Control
Tools

Actions
Align
Appearance

6.

Transform ◇ **Align** Pathfinder

Align Objects:

Distribute Objects:

7.

● LOGO 4

ONCE YOU START TO COMBINE SHAPES IT'S POSSIBLE TO CREATE A VARIETY OF INTERESTING LOGOS. THE SHAPE YOU'LL CREATE HERE WILL FORM THE BASIS FOR OTHER LOGOS THAT WILL FOLLOW.

1. Follow the steps of either of the earlier tutorials to re-create logo 2.

2. From the **Window menu** choose *Pathfinder* to show the Pathfinder panel. Pathfinder commands are used to combine shapes in different ways, for example by adding them together or subtracting them from each other.

3. With both shapes selected, press the *Intersect button,* the third from the left in the top row. This keeps only the areas of the selected shapes that overlap, and deletes everything else*.

* *In versions of Illustrator prior to CS4 you will need to press the Expand button on the right of the Pathfinder Panel to finish the process of intersecting the shapes.*

1.

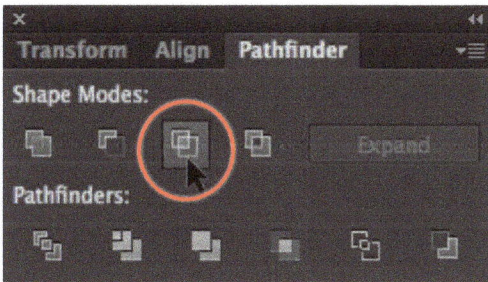

2.

3.

⊘ LOGO 5

THIS LOGO IS VERY SIMILAR TO THE PREVIOUS ONE, BUT BUILDS ON THE FEATURE YOU DISCOVERED IN THE FIRST LOGO, THAT OF TRANSFORMING A COPY OF THE SHAPE.

1. Either recreate or copy and paste the previous logo.

2. Ensuring the shape is selected, double-click on the **Rotate Tool** and rotate the shape -45 degrees.

3. Ensuring the shape is still selected, double-click on the *Scale Tool.* Like the Rotate Tool, you can either use it to transform the existing shape or to make a transformed copy of it. Enter *60* next to *Uniform* at the top of the dialogue box and press the *Copy button.* A copy of the shape that is 60% size of the original is placed over the top of the original shape (as it's the same colour, it's currently not easy to see).

4. Press the **Fill button** in the **Tools Panel** and change the fill colour of the new shape to white* by clicking on the *white* swatch in the **Swatches panel.**

* *In this case we want to make the fill of the inside white. When you reach logo 9 you will look at some approaches you could use if you had wanted to remove the inside fill to make it transparent.*

1.

Rotate

Rotate

Angle: -45°

Options: ✓ Transform Objects ☐ Transform Patterns

☑ Preview

2.

Scale

Scale

● Uniform: 60%

○ Non-Uniform

Horizontal: 60%

Vertical: 60%

3.

Options

☐ Scale Strokes & Effects

✓ Transform Objects ☐ Transform Patterns

✓ Preview

Copy   Cancel   OK

4.

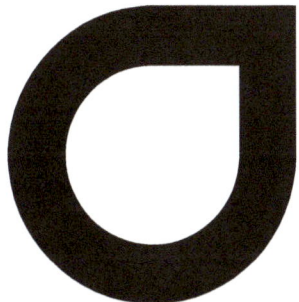

⌘ LOGO 6

BUILDING ON THE PREVIOUS LOGO, THIS SHOWS ANOTHER
WAY OF USING THE ROTATE TOOL TO MAKE A MORE
COMPLEX TRANSFORMATION TO THE SHAPE.

1. Start by making a copy of the previous logo. Ensure that
    both shapes are still selected before continuing.

2. Choose the **Rotate Tool.** You might recall that when you have
    used the Rotate Tool previously, when you double-clicked
    on it the shape was automatically rotated whilst keeping its
    centre in place. Illustrator's term for this place is the *Point
    of Origin* – and by default it's in the centre of a shape.

3. However for this logo the aim is to create a copy of the shape
    that's rotated around its top-right anchor point. For this to happen
    you need to make Illustrator work in a way different to its default
    setting. Still using the **Rotate Tool,** hold down the ***Alt key*** as
    you click on the anchor point at the top-right of the shape.

4. In the dialogue box that appears, enter *90* next to *Angle*
    and press the **Copy button.** This leaves the original shape
    in place, but creates a copy rotated at the desired angle,
    around the point of origin that you have specified.

5. To complete the logo you'll need to repeat the above
    process another two times. A quicker way to do this is
    to press the ***Command+D key**** twice. This is a shortcut
    for ***Object>Transform>Transform Again,*** a command
    that repeats exactly the last transformation (such as
    a scale, move or copy) that Illustrator made.

*   **Ctrl+D** *if you're using a PC*

1.

3.

Rotate

Rotate

Angle: 90°

Options: ✓ Transform Objects ☐ Transform Patterns

✓ Preview

Copy   Cancel   OK

4.

Object	Type	Select	Effect	View	Window	Help

Transform ►   Transform Again   ⌘D

Arrange ►

Group   ⌘G   Move...   ⇧⌘M
Ungroup   ⇧⌘G   Rotate...
Lock   ►   Reflect...
Unlock All   ⌥⌘2   Scale...
Hide   ►   Shear...
Show All   ⌥⌘3

Expand...   Transform Each... ⌥⇧⌘D

Reset Bounding Box

5.

↳ LOGO 7

IN THIS LOGO YOU'LL USE AN ALTERNATIVE APPROACH
TO PATHFINDER TO DIVIDE OBJECTS AND DISCOVER
A WAY TO CUT AWAY PARTS OF AN OBJECT.

1. Recreate a copy of logo 1. Change the **fill** colour of one of the shapes so you can which of the rounded rectangles is in front of the other. If the tall shape appears to be behind the wide shape, select it and choose *Arrange>Bring to Front* from the **Object menu.**

2. With the tall shape still selected, choose *Path>Divide Objects Below* from the **Object menu.**

3. It's hard to see what's happened, so in the **Tools Panel** press the *Swap Fill and Stroke button:* now the fill takes on the colour that the stroke had, and vice-versa. As you can see, the tall shape has disappeared and has left the wide shape, but divided at the point where they had previously overlapped.

4. With the **Selection Tool** click on an empty part of the page to deselect all the shapes. Click on the stroke of the middle shape to select it (because it has no fill, clicking where the fill would be will have no effect). Press the *Delete key* to delete it, leaving the two end shapes.

5. In the **Tools Panel** press and hold down on the *Eraser Tool* until the other tools appear from beneath it. Choose the *Scissors Tool.* Click once each on the four innermost anchor points to separate the two vertical lines from the rest of the shapes.

6. Choose the **Selection Tool** and click on an empty part of the page, then click on each vertical line in turn and remove it by pressing the **Delete key.** If the final result doesn't look like diagram 6, choose **Undo** from the **Edit menu** a few times to go back, and try again.

7. Align the ends of the two lines together using either of the features you learned about when creating logo 2.

8. From the **Window menu** choose *Stroke.* In the *Stroke Panel* increase the stroke *Weights* to about *6pt.* To finish, **rotate** the logo by *-90* degrees.

A logo that's created using strokes is usually "outlined" upon completion. You'll learn about this in the next tutorial.

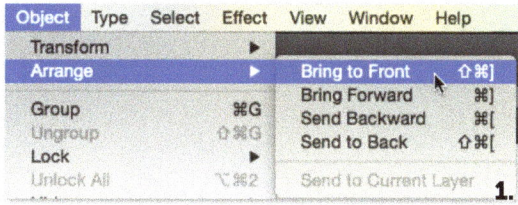

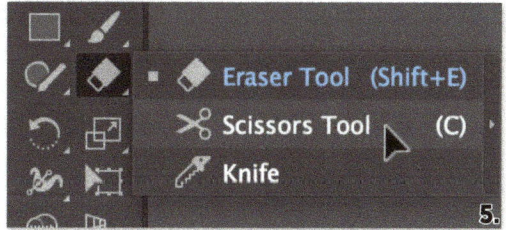

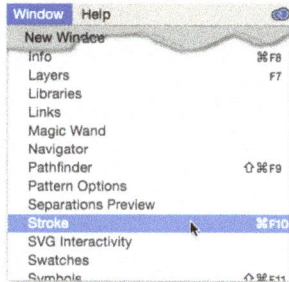

⊗ LOGO 8

IN THE PROCESS OF CREATING THIS LOGO YOU'LL
DISCOVER ANOTHER PATHFINDER FEATURE, AND LEARN
HOW TO CONVERT A STROKE INTO A FILL.

1. Recreate a copy of logo 1.

2. Currently the logo has a fill of *black* and a stroke of *none*. In the
    Tools Panel press the **Swap Fill and Stroke button:** now the
    fill takes on the colour that the stroke had, and vice-versa.

3. Now that the rectangles have a stroke but no fill, you can
    see clearly that they are two separate objects. To create
    the final logo the two shapes need to be combined, so that
    the stroke runs around the edge of one single shape.

4. To combine the shapes, make sure they are both selected and
    press the *Unite button* on the top left of the **Pathfinder Panel*.**

5. Using the **Rotate Tool,** rotate the shape *45* degrees
    and increase the **Stroke weight** to about *6pt.*

6. Once a logo like this is finished it's common practice to convert the
    strokes to *outlines.* The strokes are then re-created as if they were
    filled objects. This finalises the process, making it impossible to
    accidentally make it thicker or thinner later (which might be just what
    you want once a logo's design has been finalised). To do this, from
    the **Object menu** choose *Path>Outline Stroke.* It is good practice
    to save a copy of the logo before you convert the strokes to outlines,
    in case you want to go back and make any changes to it later**.

* *In versions of Illustrator prior to CS4 you will need to press the Expand button on the
    right of the Pathfinder Panel to finish the process of combining the shapes.*

** *Some of the logos you've already created, and most of those that follow are
    made of strokes, so consider using this approach on these logos too.*

1.

2.

3.

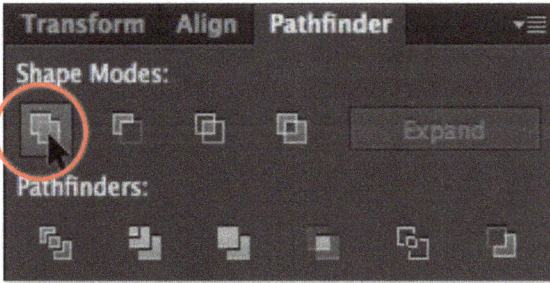

4.

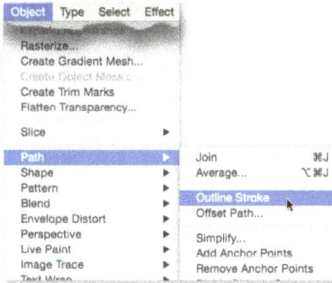

5.

6.

LOGO 9

DURING THE PROCESS OF CREATING THIS LOGO YOU'LL DISCOVER A MUCH MORE FLEXIBLE WAY TO DIVIDE SHAPES FROM EACH OTHER, AND LEARN HOW TO WORK WITH OBJECTS THAT ARE GROUPED.

1. Create a Rounded Rectangle of *7mm Width, 20mm Height, and 4mm Corner Radius.* Give it a *black* stroke of *2pt* and a fill of *none.*

2. As you did when creating logo 6, choose the **Rotate Tool,** and hold down the **alt key** as you click on the shape's bottom anchor point. Enter an angle of *90* and press **Copy** to rotate a copy around the bottom of the shape.

3. Repeat the process another two times using either the **Command+D** shortcut or by choosing **Transform>Transform Again** from the **Object menu.**

4. Making sure all the shapes are selected, press the ***Divide button*** on the bottom-left of the **Pathfinder Panel*.** Whilst the logo might not look very different yet, at every point where the shapes intersected, they have been divided.

5. To create the final logo you will need to delete the four outer shapes and leave the inner four. If you try to do this using the **Selection Tool** you will find that when you click on any one shape you will select them all. This is because when you perform certain tasks (including Pathfinder commands) Illustrator creates a *Group* – and the Selection Tool always selects whole groups. So to select objects inside the group you will need to use the *Group Selection Tool* instead. In the **Tools Panel** press down on the **Direct Selection Tool** and when the ***Group Selection Tool*** appears, select it.

6. Click on a blank area of the page to deselect all the shapes. Then carefully select any shapes you want to remove (remember that as they have no fill, you'll need to click on their stroke to select them), and press the **Delete key** until you are left with the final shapes.

7. From the **Object menu** choose **Path>Outline Stroke** to finish the logo.

* *Since Illustrator CS5 the Shape Builder Tool can be used instead of the Pathfinder Panel to create this logo and those that follow it. You'll learn about this in the next tutorial.*

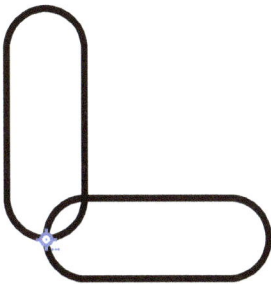
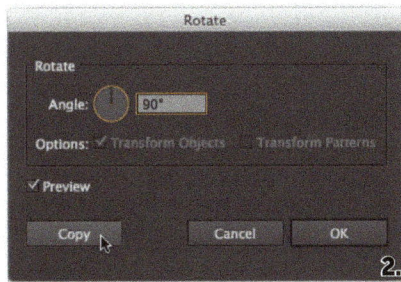

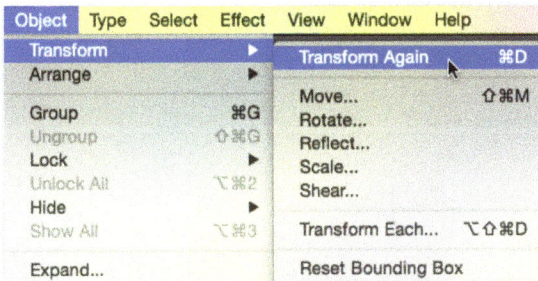
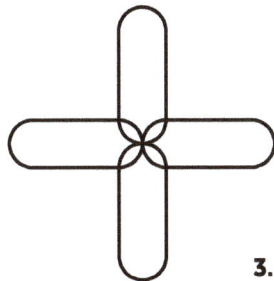

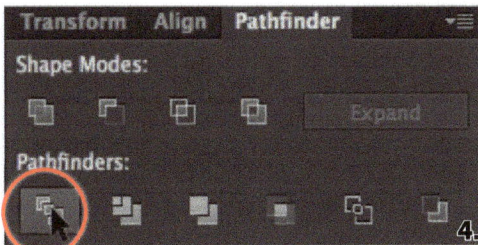

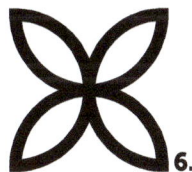

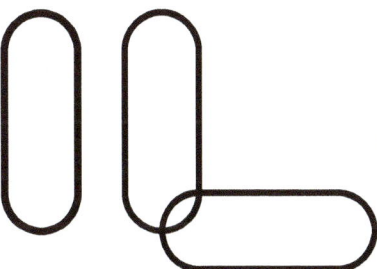

LOGO 9 [CS5 onwards]

AN ALTERNATIVE WAY TO CREATE THE PREVIOUS LOGO (AND ALL OF THE LOGOS THAT FOLLOW THAT USE PATHFINDER COMMANDS) IS TO USE THE SHAPE BUILDER TOOL THAT APPEARED IN ILLUSTRATOR CS5.

1. Follow the first three steps in the previous tutorial to create the four overlapping rounded rectangles.

2. Using the **Selection Tool,** select all the rectangles. Choose the ***Shape Builder Tool*** from the **Tools Panel.**

3. Notice that when you hover the **Shape Builder Tool** over the different parts of the shapes it indicates where they could be split up by highlighting them.

4. Hold down the **Alt key** and notice that the 'plus' changes to a 'minus', indicating that the Shape Builder Tool can delete this area. Delete the all the outer shapes by keeping down the **Alt key** and clicking on each one in turn.

5. From the **Object menu** choose **Path>Outline Stroke** to finish the logo.

1.

2.

3.

4.

⚘ LOGO 10

FOR THIS LOGO YOU'LL LEARN A MORE FLEXIBLE WAY TO
CREATE A ROUNDED RECTANGLE, AND COMBINE A REPEATED
TRANSFORMATION WITH PATHFINDER OR SHAPE BUILDER.

1. With the **Rounded Rectangle Tool** click and drag on the page. Without releasing the mouse button, hold down the *Left arrow key* and notice that the rectangle's corners become fully square.

2. Still without releasing the mouse button, hold down the *Right arrow key* and notice that the rectangle's corners become fully rounded.

3. With the mouse button still down, press the *Down arrow key* repeatedly and notice how the corners become gradually less rounded; the opposite is true if you do the same with the *Up arrow key.* Experiment until you get a shape you're happy with, then let go of the mouse button*. Apply a fill of *none* and a stroke of *black.*

4. Choose the **Selection Tool** and select the shape by clicking on its edge. Hold down the **alt key** and drag the shape, and notice that instead of moving the original shape, you are dragging a copy of it. Keep the **alt key** held down until you've released your mouse button to create a copy of the shape. Adjust the position of the new shape, considering that the outer shapes will soon be discarded, leaving only the central shape where the objects overlap.

5. Select both shapes. On the **Pathfinder Panel** press the *Intersect button***, the third button from the left on the top row. This keeps the area where the shapes overlap and discards the rest.

6. Choose the **Rotate Tool.** Hold down the **alt key** as you click on the shape's bottom right anchor point. In the dialogue box that appears rotate a copy of the shape by *90* degrees.

7. Create two more rotated copies by pressing **Command+D** twice.

8. From the **Object menu** choose **Path>Outline Stroke** to finish the logo.

* *In CC you may also see blue circles inside the shape. Dragging these is another way to adjust roundedness.*

** *In versions of Illustrator prior to CS4 you will need to press the Expand button on the right of the Pathfinder Panel to finish the process of combining the shapes. Since version CS5 you could alternatively use the Shape Builder Tool here.* **96–97**

1.

2.

3.

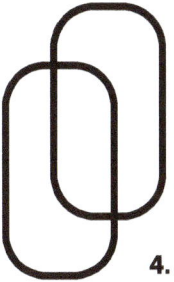
4.

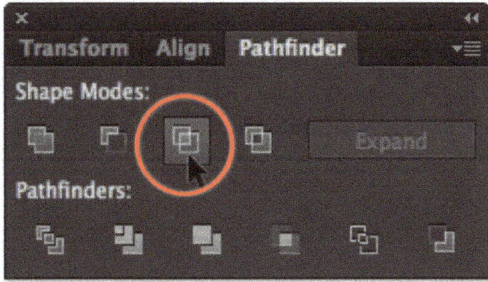
5.

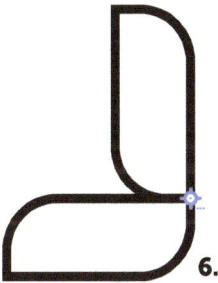
6.

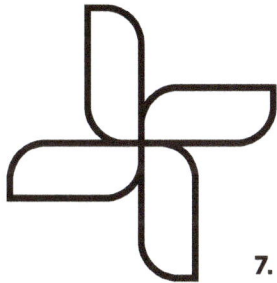
7.

◈ LOGO 11

THIS LOGO IS A LOT SIMPLER TO CREATE THAN IT MIGHT
APPEAR – IT IS SIMPLY FOUR ROUNDED RECTANGLES
ROTATED AND ARRANGED IN A SQUARE.

1. Create a rounded rectangle with a thick *black* stroke and a fill of
    none. Using the **Rotate Tool,** rotate the shape by *45* degrees.

2. Using the **Selection Tool,** hold down the **alt key**
    and drag the rectangle to create a copy.

3. Select both shapes and double-click on the **Rotate
    Tool.** Enter *90* degrees and press the **Copy button** to
    create the four shapes you want, roughly aligned.

4. Using either of the techniques described in logo 2, align the four
    shapes accurately by their anchor points to create the final shape.

5. If you want to check whether your shapes are in fact properly
    aligned, choose *Outline* from the **View menu.** This shows just the
    bare bones of the shapes, and can be really useful when you want
    a clearer picture of what you're doing*. To change the view back,
    go back to the same place in the **View menu** and choose *Preview.*

6. From the **Object menu** choose **Path>Outline
    Stroke** to finish the logo.

* *It's possible to work in Outline mode, but if you are, you can only select shapes by their edges or their centres.*

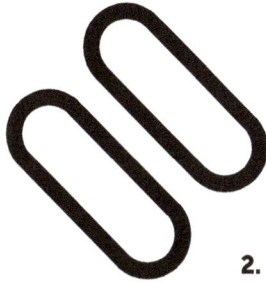
1.

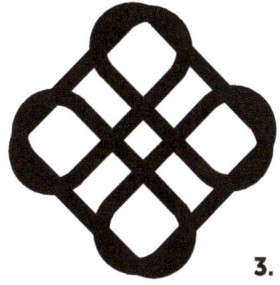
2.

3.

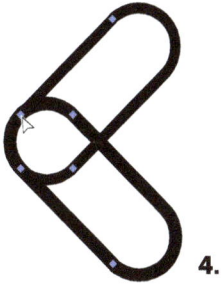
4.

View   Window   Help

Outline   ⌘Y

Overprint Preview   ⌥⇧⌘Y
Pixel Preview   ⌥⌘Y

Proof Setup   ▶
Proof Colors

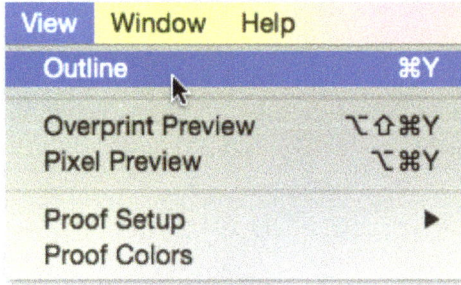
5.

6.

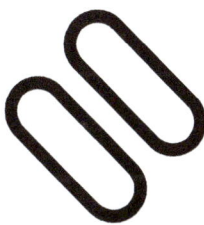

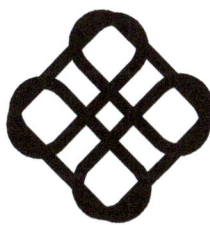

✳ LOGO 12

THE FINAL LOGO INTRODUCES THE CONCEPT OF APPEARANCE, THE
ABILITY OF A SHAPE TO HAVE MORE COMPLEX PROPERTIES THAN
USUAL – IN THIS CASE ONE STROKE ON TOP OF THE OTHER.

1. Create a rounded rectangle by clicking and dragging with
   the **Rounded Rectangle Tool** in combination with the arrow
   keys. Apply a fill of *none* and a *4pt* width *black* stroke.

2. Double-click on the **Rotate Tool** and create a copy
   rotated *90* degrees around the centre of the shape.

3. Select both shapes with the **Selection tool** and use either
   the **Unite button** on the **Pathfinder Panel** or the **Shape
   Builder Tool** to combine the two shapes into one.

4. In the **Stroke Panel** click on the *Round Join* corner button
   to make the inner corners rounded instead of square.

5. Locate the *Appearance Panel* towards the bottom right of your screen
   (if it is not showing, choose *Appearance* from the **Window menu**). In
   the **Appearance Panel** click the *Add New Stroke button* on its bottom
   left corner. This adds a virtual stroke on top of your original (real) one.

6. Notice that the additional stroke is highlighted in the **Appearance
   Panel,** and that if you click on the word *Stroke,* (or the colour or
   weight) they reveal popup menus. Using these pop-up menus adjust
   the topmost stroke so that it is a *white* stroke of *0.25pt* weight.

7. To finish the logo, double-click on the **Rotate Tool** again,
   this time creating a copy rotated around *45* degrees.

8. If you want to create an outlined version of the logo you'll firstly
   need to *expand* the appearance to turn the virtual strokes into real
   ones. To do this, select the shapes and choose *Expand Appearance*
   from the **Object menu.** You may need to ungroup the objects by
   choosing *Object>Ungroup* before creating outlines in the usual way.

1.

2.

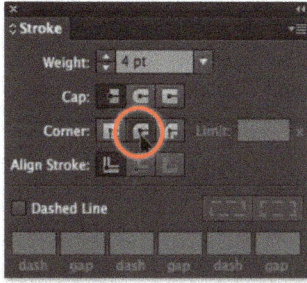

3.

4.

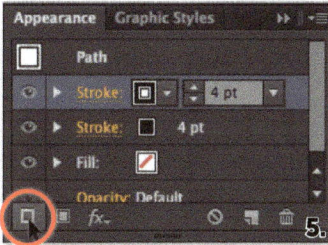

5.

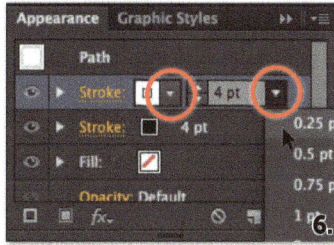

6.

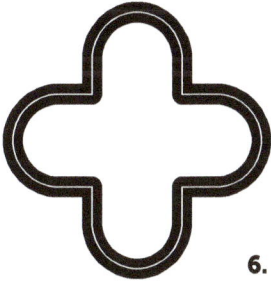

6.

7.

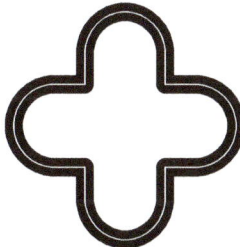

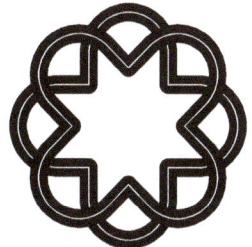

LECO 1976

BEBAS NEUE

LEAGUE GOTHI

RANGE

Learning Curve Pro

Otama.ep

Museo 70

VAL BOLD

Sofia Regular

Lobster Two

Creating Logos from Type

ABOUT THE TYPE

All the typefaces used for these logos have been made by designers who have generously made them freely available for anyone to use. I'd recommend downloading and installing them all before you start working on the logos. If you're a user Typekit, the typefaces shown in bold are also available there.

These fonts are free to download from www.fontsquirrel.com

Bebas Neue – *Flat-It* – *www.dharmatype.com/flat-it*

Sofia – *Latinotype* – *www.latinotype.com*

Pincoyablack – *Daniel Hernandez* – *www.latinotype.com*

Learning Curve Pro – *Blue Vinyl Fonts* – *www.bvfonts.com*

Lobster – *Pablo Impallari* – *www.impallari.com*

Otama e.p. – *Tim Donaldson* – *www.otamatypeface.com*

These fonts are free to download from www.myfonts.com

Museo 700 – *Jos Buivenga* – *Exljbris* – *www.exljbris.com*

Leco 1976 – *Samuel Carnoky* – *Carnoky Type* – *www.carnoky.com*

These fonts are free to download direct from their creators:

Val Bold – *Font Fabric* – *www.fontfabric.com/val-font*

League Gothic – *League of Moveable Type* –
   www.theleagueofmoveabletype.com

You are invited to make a donation for these Lost Type Co-op fonts:

Ranger – *Evan Huwa* – *Lost Type Co-op* – *www.losttype.com*

Airship – *James George Dunn* –*Lost Type Co-op* – *www.losttype.com*

TEXT FORMATTING

BEFORE YOU START TO CREATE LOGOS, HERE IS A BRIEF INTRODUCTION TO BASIC TEXT FORMATTING THAT YOU CAN APPLY IN ILLUSTRATOR. IF YOU ARE ALREADY FAMILIAR WITH THIS, SKIP TO THE FIRST LOGO.

1. From the **File menu** choose **New** to create a new document. In the dialogue box that appears, choose *Print* from the available options, change the *Size* to *Tabloid* and press the **Create button.**

2. In the **Tools Panel** click once on the **Type Tool** (that resembles a "T"). Click anywhere on the page, and you'll see a flashing cursor appear, possibly along with some dummy text. Type the word "Text".

3. Notice that the **Control Panel** near the top of the screen now contains information about the text you're working with. It probably tells you that the **Font** you're using is *Myriad Pro,* the **Style** of the typeface is *Regular* and the **Size** of the type is *12pt* (these are Illustrator's defaults).

Myriad Pro | Regular | 12 pt

3.

Character: Ranger | Regular | 72 pt

5.

4. As the text is currently quite small it's hard to read. To make it larger, firstly you have to select the type. Drag back through the text with the **Type Tool** to select it and notice that it becomes highlighted. Then in the **Control Panel** click on the drop down arrow to the right of the (12pt) *Font Size* and change the Font **Size** to *72pt.* Change the **Font** to *Ranger Regular* (for details on how to download it, see the start of the book).

5. Whilst you can easily change the Font, Style and Size of type easily in the Control Panel, if you want to change other attributes of the text you'll need to use the *Character Panel.* There are three ways to get access to make this appear. The first way is to click on the word "Character" in the Control Panel. The second is to choose *Type>Character* from the *Window menu.* The third is to use a keyboard shortcut, *Command +T (Ctrl+T on PC).*

6. In the **Character panel** as well as changing the font, its style and weight you have access to other aspects such as *tracking* and *kerning.* If you have previously worked with type it's likely you'll be familiar with these terms, and if you've used InDesign then you'll recognise the symbols here and what they mean. If that's the case then you might want to skip to the first logo.

7. **Tracking** is the space between a series of characters. To see this in action, with your text selected, change the tracking to *50* and see that whilst the size of the text does not change, it takes up more space because there's now more space between each character. Change the tracking to *-75* and notice that there is now less space between each character.

8. **Kerning** is like tracking, but only applies to a *pair* of letters. To see this in action, click once with your *Type Tool* between the "x" and the "t" of the word "Text". Your cursor flashes slowly to let you know where it is. Notice that the two characters are almost touching. Look at the **Kerning field** in the Character Panel. The number is the kerning value for that pair of letters when using that font. If you see brackets, they indicate that the value has been automatically applied. Using the dropdown arrow on the right, change the kerning value to *50* and you should notice the characters become a little less close. If you want more refined control of the kerning or tracking, either use the up and down arrows to the left of the values, or type a value directly into the field.

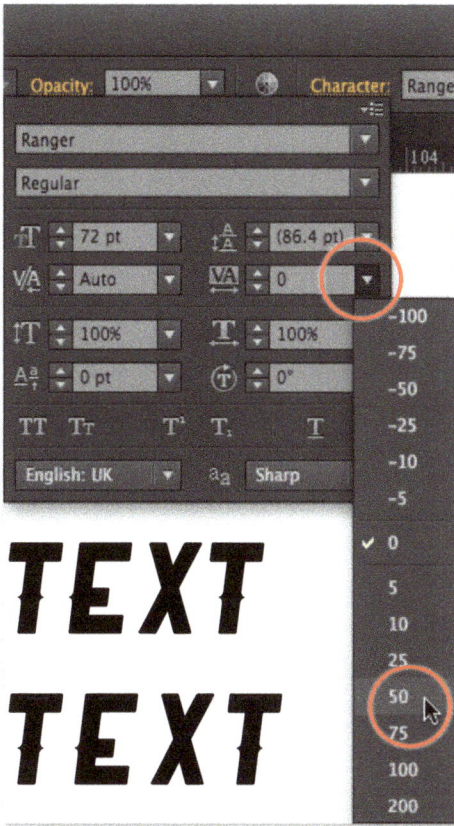

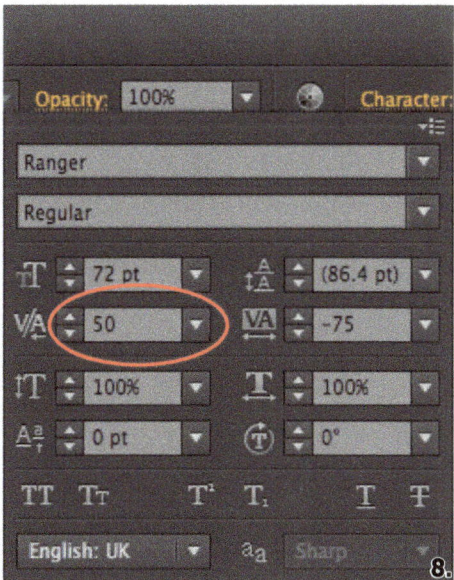

RANGER

IN THE PROCESS OF CREATING THIS FIRST LOGO YOU'LL
MAKE SOME BASIC CHANGES TO THE TYPE'S FILL AND
STROKE AND LEARN A QUICK WAY TO DUPLICATE TEXT.

1. From the **File menu** choose **New** to create a new document.
    In the dialogue box that appears, choose *Print* from the
    available options, change the *Size* to *Tabloid* and press the
    Create button. You'll create all your logos in this document*.
    As this document is *Tabloid* size, it's a lot bigger than the logos
    you'll create. So shortly you'll learn how to zoom in, out and
    around the page to see what you need to be looking at.

2. From the **Tools Panel** select the **Type Tool** and click once on the page.

3. A flashing cursor appears, (possibly with some dummy text alongside
    it) expecting you to type. Type *"RANGER"*. As described previously,
    drag back over the text to select it. Then change the font to *Ranger
    Regular* (you'll need to download and install this and all the fonts
    used in this book – see the start of the book) and the size to *72pt*.

4. Before you go any further it might be useful to have a closer
    view of what you're doing. To see your work larger on the
    screen, hold down the **Command key** and press the **+ key** to
    zoom in. If you've zoomed in and you want to change which
    part of the screen you're looking at, either use the document's
    scroll bars, or from the **Tools Panel** choose the **Hand Tool**
    and drag with your mouse to reposition the screen**.

5. Next you'll do rotate the text so that instead of being slanted, it rises
    diagonally from left to right. To help with this process you'll make
    use of a *Guide*. From the **Tools Panel** choose the **Selection Tool.**

6. From the **View menu** choose **Rulers>Show Rulers.**

7. Click on the ruler to the left of the page and drag a guide onto the
    page, roughly aligned with the bottom left of the *"N"* in your text. »

---

* *There are a couple of alternative approaches you could take instead of creating one large
   document. These are discussed towards the end of the Brief Technical Notes section.*

** *To zoom back out again, hold down the Command key and press the – key. To see the whole screen,
   hold down the Command key and press the 0 (zero) key. Instead of selecting the Hand Tool to scroll
   the screen you can alternatively hold down the Spacebar key – but this is not advisable when you are
   using the Type Tool, as it will either insert spaces in the text or delete it instead of scrolling the page.*

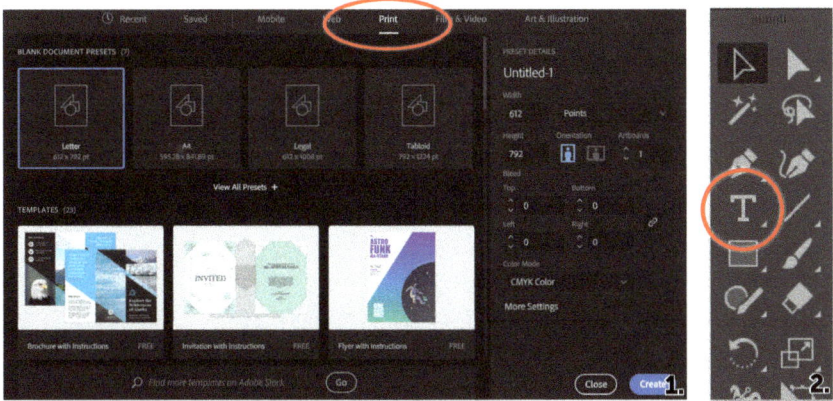

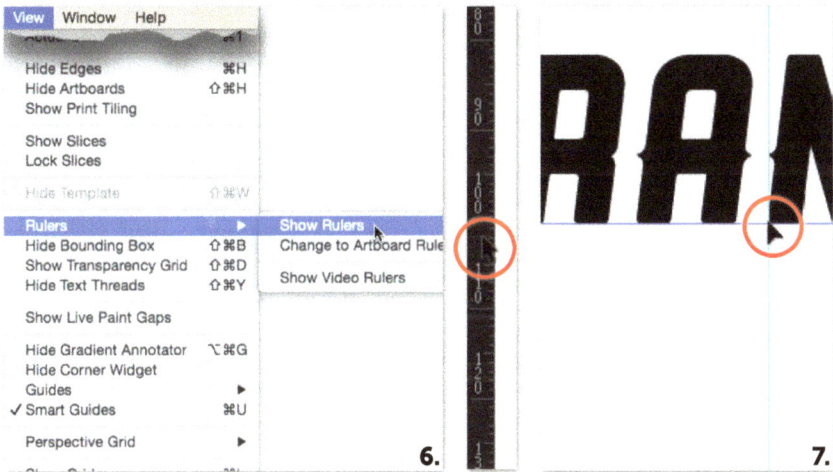

8. Look closely at your text. You should see that it's surrounded by a thin blue rectangle with small blue squares at each corner. This is the *Bounding Box,* and it indicates that your text is selected, meaning it's the object that Illustrator is currently working with. If you don't see the bounding box, click back onto the text with the **Selection Tool.**

9. From the **Tools Panel** double-click on the *Rotate Tool.* When the dialogue box appears, ensure that the *Preview box* is checked and drag over the text that describes the angle of rotation (which should be *0°).* Press the *up arrow* on your keyboard to gradually increase the angle of rotation until the flat edge of the "N" is parallel to the guide you've just drawn (roughly *7* degrees). Press the **OK button.**

10. Remove the guide you previously drew by choosing *Guides>Clear Guides* from the *View menu.*

11. From the **Tools Panel** choose the **Selection Tool.** Hold down the *Alt key* as you drag your text a little way. By holding down the Alt key you will create a copy of the text instead of moving the original.

12. Your newly copied text will look the same as the first: it has a black *fill* and no *stroke.* To change it to look like the final logo in the step diagram at the foot of the following page, firstly locate the *Fill button* that's towards the bottom of the **Tools Panel** and click on it – this enables you to change the fill colour.

13. To make the text's fill white, firstly locate the button near the top right of your screen used to reveal the *Swatches Panel,* and click on it. From the swatches that have appeared, click on the *white* one near the panel's top left.

14. In the **Tools Panel** click on the *Stroke button** that's next to the Fill button. Make the text's stroke black by clicking on the *black* swatch near the top left of the **Swatches Panel**. »

---

* What I have described as the Fill and Stroke buttons are not strictly buttons, but the areas you click to bring either the fill or stroke to the front, determining which will change when you apply a swatch.

** In Illustrator CC or CS6 you might find that at this point that the Swatches panel closes, and the Color panel opens. Whilst the Swatches panel is normally preferred when applying colours, you can apply black, white or none just as easily using the Colour panel.

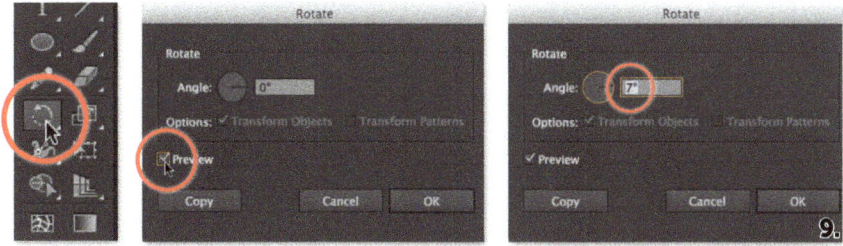

8.

9.

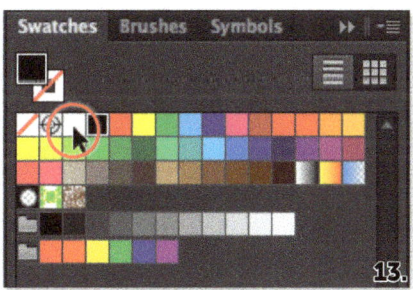

11.

12.

13.

14.

15. To see what your logo really looks like you'll need to deselect it. Currently the topmost type is selected, meaning that Illustrator knows that you're working with it, and anything that you do will affect it. You can hopefully see it's selected because you can see the Bounding Box that surrounds it. To deselect it, firstly choose the **Selection Tool** from the top of the **Tools Panel.** Then simply click on an empty part of the page.

16. If you want to reposition the text, click and drag it with the **Selection Tool** to move it to a new location.

RANGER

15.

SOFIA

IN THE COURSE OF CREATING THIS LOGO YOU'LL LEARN HOW TO CONVERT TEXT TO OUTLINES, COMBINE PATHS AND HOW TO CREATE A DASHED LINE AROUND THE EDGE OF THE TEXT.

1. Continue working in the same document. Like other programs you'll have used, you can save files easily in Illustrator: choose *Save* from the **File menu** if you want to save your document (options will appear – stick with the default settings). Reposition the screen with the *Hand Tool* or use the **Command –** shortcut if you want to give yourself more space to work in.

2. From the **Tools Panel** select the **Type Tool** and click once on the page.

3. When you see the flashing cursor, type *"Sofia"*. The text that appears will be of the same typeface and size you last used, which is probably 72pt Ranger Regular.

4. From the **Tools Panel** choose the **Selection Tool***. Notice the Bounding Box surrounding the text, indicating that it's selected. Look in the **Control Panel** towards the top of the screen and notice that even though you're no longer using the Type Tool, information about the text is still displayed. Click on the *Character* button, change the font to *Sofia Regular* and the size to *60pt.*

5. The finished logo will have a fill of *none* and a stroke of *black,* but currently it's the opposite way round, with a *black* fill and no stroke. To quickly swap these colours over, press the *Swap fill and stroke button* towards the bottom of the **Tools panel.**

6. The look of the text you've worked with so far has been defined by the font itself. This means that you could retype the text, change the font, point size or any other character attribute. Whilst this is flexible, it can only take you so far. You can do much more with the text if you can work directly with its *anchor points,* which is the way most of the remaining logos in this book will be created. To do this, make sure you're using the **Selection Tool** and that your text is selected, and choose *Create Outlines* from the **Type menu. »**

*   *Once you have finished typing the text you want, it's generally easier to work with the Selection Tool from then on.*

SOFIA. 3.

Sofia. 4.

Sofia. 5.

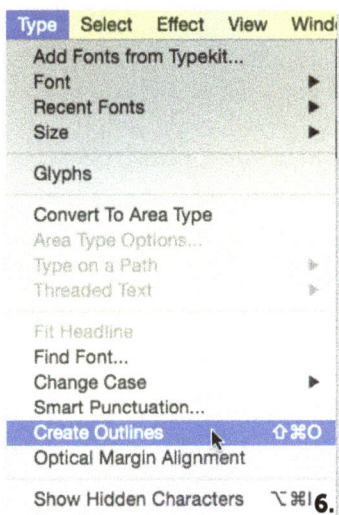

7. Now you've converted your text to outlines, you should see that rather than having one anchor point it now has dozens*. It is now effectively no longer text – you couldn't retype it**. When logos that include type are finished, the text will invariably be converted to outlines. This is partly for creative reasons, partly to help protect the brand, and also that it ensures that the logo can be displayed correctly anywhere, and not just seen by people who have that font installed on their computer.

8. If you look carefully at where the "i" meets the "a" you should see that there is an overlap. As the effect you're going to create will resemble a line of stitches around the edge of the text, it won't work if there are any overlaps. To combine the letters into one shape, firstly choose **Pathfinder** from the **Window menu.** Pathfinder commands are used to combine shapes in different ways, for example by adding them together or subtracting them from each other.

9. Make sure your text is selected (if you don't see lots of blue anchor points, choose the **Selection Tool** and click on it). Then press the **Unite button** on the top left of the **Pathfinder Panel** to combine the paths (Illustrator's term for objects).

10. To finish the logo you'll make adjustments to the text's stroke. To do this, firstly locate the **Stroke Panel** at the right of the screen, or choose **Stroke** from the **Window menu.** If the panel looks as it does in diagram 10, press the button on its very top left to reveal more options.

11. In the stroke panel, the **Weight** describes the thickness of the stroke – the default value is *1 point (1pt).* Click on the popup menu to the right of the stroke weight to adjust it to *0.5pt.* To make the stroke resemble stitching, firstly click on the **Dashed Line** checkbox. Change both the width of the **dash** and the **gap** to *1pt,* and press the **Round Cap** button to make the end of each dash rounded instead of square. To get a clearer view of what you've done, deselect the text, and if need be reselect it and make further adjustments to its stroke.

* *If you want a clearer view of your anchor points, in the View Menu choose Hide Bounding Box. Whilst this feature provides an easy way to transform objects it can also obscure your view of an object's anchor points. To turn it back on, choose Show Bounding Box, also from the View Menu.*

** *For that reason it's generally a good idea to create a copy of your text before you convert it to outlines.*

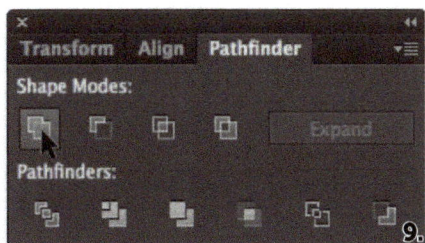

7.

9.

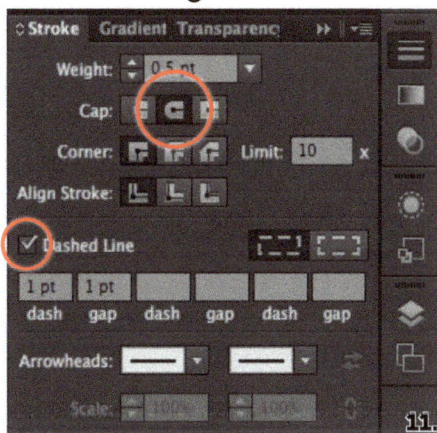

10.

11.

MUSEO 700

DURING THE CREATION OF THIS LOGO YOU'LL LEARN MORE
ABOUT MANIPULATING TYPE THAT HAS BEEN CONVERTED TO
OUTLINES. IN PARTICULAR YOU'LL LOOK AT COMPOUND PATHS.

1. Continue working in the same document. Click once on the page with the **Type Tool,** type *"Museo 700"* and change the font to *Museo 700.* Give the type a point size that you can view it at.

2. Choose the **Selection Tool** from the **Tools Panel*.** As you learnt in the previous exercise, you'll often need to convert type to outlines – do that here by choosing **Convert to Outlines** from the **Type menu.**

3. If you look carefully at your text you'll see the large number of anchor points that define the paths. Notice that the anchor points are all solid blue, which means that they are all selected. With the **Selection Tool,** click on an empty part of the page to deselect the type.

4. Choose the *Direct Selection Tool* from the **Tools Panel** and click carefully on the edge of a letter. If you click accurately, you'll see that all of the anchor points surrounding the letter are visible, but they are hollow. This means they are not currently selected, but you could select any one of them. Click carefully on the very bottom left of the letter "M" – you should notice that the anchor point becomes solid blue as you select it.

5. Hold down the *Shift key* and click on the anchor point directly above to select that as well. Then click back on either of the anchor points and start to drag to the left, reshaping the text. Try to drag in a straight line – you should notice the green *Smart Guides* appearing to help you do this.

6. Repeat this with any other (pairs of) anchor points you want to change. If you don't like the result, choose *Undo* from the *Edit menu.*

7. With the (black) **Selection Tool** click back on any part of the text. Notice how the insides of the e, o, and the 0s (known as *counters*) are defined by anchor points too. These are called *Compound Paths,* where the shape is defined both by the anchor points outside it, and those inside it too.

8. To remove the counters, choose *Compound Paths>Release* from the *Object menu.*

* *If the text is selected with the Type Tool, Create Outlines won't work.*

Museo 700. 1.

Museo 700. 3.

M 4.

M M M M 5.

anchor
X: 40.44 mm
Y: 134.75 mm

dX: -18.92 mm
dY: 0 mm

Museo700. 6. eo 7.

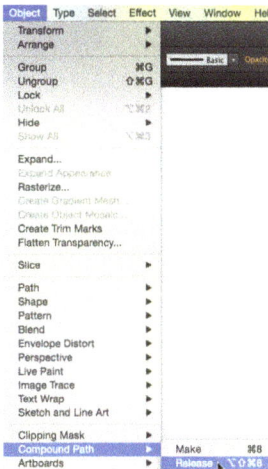

| Object | Type | Select | Effect | View | Window | Help |

Transform ▶
Arrange ▶

Group   ⌘G
Ungroup   ⇧⌘G
Lock   ▶
Unlock All   ⌥⌘2
Hide   ▶
Show All   ⌥⌘3

Expand...
Expand Appearance
Rasterize...
Create Gradient Mesh...
Create Object Mosaic...
Create Trim Marks
Flatten Transparency...

Slice   ▶

Path   ▶
Shape   ▶
Pattern   ▶
Blend   ▶
Envelope Distort ▶
Perspective   ▶
Live Paint   ▶
Image Trace   ▶
Text Wrap   ▶
Sketch and Line Art ▶

Clipping Mask   ▶
Compound Path   ▶   Make   ⌘8
Artboards   ▶   Release ⇧⌥⌘8

Museo700. 8.

PINCOYABLACK

IN THE CREATION OF THIS LOGO YOU'LL LEARN MORE ABOUT
COMPOUND PATHS, HOW TO WORK WITH GROUPS, AND IN
PARTICULAR HOW TO USE THE GROUP SELECTION TOOL.

1. In the same way as you have done before, create *72pt* sized text with
    Pincoyablack. Convert it to outlines. In the previous exercise you
    removed the holes in the type by releasing the compound paths. If
    you click carefully back on that text you'll see that the shapes defining
    the counters are still there. This time you'll learn not only how to
    remove them, but also how to replace them with a different shape.

2. In the **Tools Panel** click on the *Rectangle Tool* and
    keep the mouse button held down until other tools
    appear from beneath it. Choose the *Star Tool.*

3. Click and drag from the centre of the counter in the letter P to create
    a star. The further you drag, the larger the star will be*. If you don't
    get the effect you wanted, choose **Undo** from the **Edit menu** and try
    again. Use the **Command +** shortcut if you need to get a closer view.

4. Change the fill colour of the star to *red* so that you can clearly
    see it against both the black and white. As you have done
    previously, use the **Selection Tool** in combination with the **Alt
    key** to drag copies of the star over the other small counters.

5. To finish the logo you'll select and delete the original counters, but if
    you try to do this using the **Selection Tool** you'll find that when you click
    on any one shape you'll select them all. This is because a compound
    path is technically a *Group* – and the Selection Tool always selects
    whole groups. To select objects inside a group you'll use the *Group
    Selection Tool* instead. In the **Tools Panel** press down on the **Direct
    Selection Tool** and when the **Group Selection Tool** appears, select it.

6. Using the **Group Selection Tool,** click on an empty part of the
    page to deselect everything. Then carefully click on the counter
    of the "P") to select it, then press the *Delete key* to remove it.

7. Using the same technique, delete the counter of the letter "o". »

* *Whilst still dragging the mouse, should you wish your star to have more or less
  points, press either the **Up** or **Down arrow** key to increase or reduce them.*

Rectangle Tool (M)
Rounded Rectangle Tool
Ellipse Tool (L)
Polygon Tool
Star Tool
Flare Tool

2.

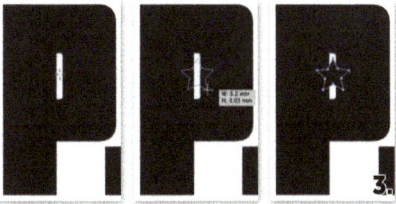

3.

4.

Direct Selection Tool (A)
Group Selection Tool

5.

6.

7.

8. The counters of the other letters may be harder to delete because you might not be able to see them underneath the stars that you've drawn. So you can see more clearly, from the very top of the **View menu** choose *Outline.* As *Outline mode* shows only the bare bones of the shapes it can make it much easier to see what's happening when viewing complex artwork.

9. Using the **Group Selection tool,** click carefully on the *edge* of each of the remaining original counters to select them, and delete them.

10. To leave Outline mode, choose *Preview* from the very top of the **View menu.**

11. Finally, select all the shapes* and choose *Compound Path>Make* from the **Object menu** to remake the shapes with the star shaped counters.

* *A good way to do this is to click with your Selection Tool a distance away from everything, then click and drag with it over all the shapes. You'll notice a faint rectangle appear which indicates what will be selected. Make sure the rectangle either encloses or touches everything you want selected (but nothing that you don't), and let your mouse button go to select everything at once*

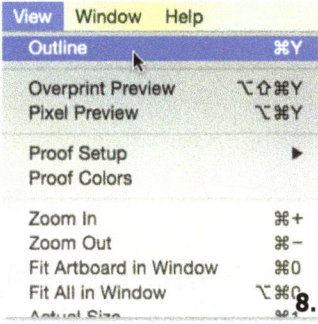

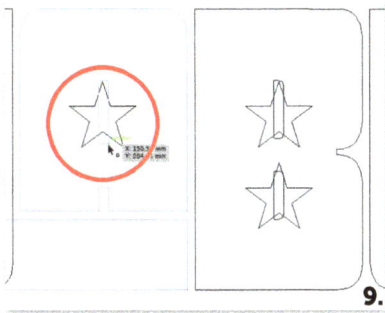

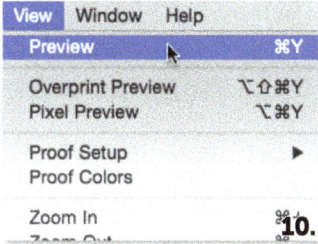

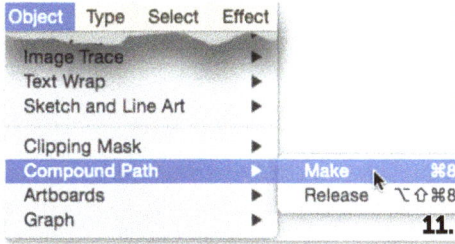

View Window Help

Outline	⌘Y
Overprint Preview	⌥⇧⌘Y
Pixel Preview	⌥⌘Y
Proof Setup	▶
Proof Colors	
Zoom In	⌘+
Zoom Out	⌘−
Fit Artboard in Window	⌘0
Fit All in Window	⌥⌘0
Actual Size	⌘1

8.

9.

View Window Help

Preview	⌘Y
Overprint Preview	⌥⇧⌘Y
Pixel Preview	⌥⌘Y
Proof Setup	▶
Proof Colors	
Zoom In	⌘+

10.

Object Type Select Effect

Image Trace	▶
Text Wrap	▶
Sketch and Line Art	▶
Clipping Mask	▶
Compound Path	▶	Make	⌘8
Artboards	▶	Release	⌥⇧⌘8
Graph	▶

11.

AIRSHIP-27

FOR THIS LOGO YOU'LL EXPLORE SOME OF ILLUSTRATOR'S
ENVELOPE DISTORT COMMANDS, INCLUDING THE ABILITY
TO TRANSFORM THE TEXT USING ANOTHER OBJECT.

1. As you have done previously, create *72pt* sized text with *Airship–27.*
   Change to the **Selection Tool,** but *don't* convert the text to outlines.

2. From the **Object menu** choose *Envelope Distort* and choose *Make
   with Warp.* These are some preset distortions that you can apply to
   anything, and can often work well with text. However we're going to
   explore a different option which often has more creative potential.

3. If you've applied any settings to your text, choose **Undo** from
   the **Edit menu.** Deselect your text. You're going to create a
   custom shape to distort the text with. In the **Tools Panel** click on
   the **Star Tool** and keep the mouse button held down until other
   tools appear from beneath it. Choose the *Rectangle Tool.*

4. Using the **Fill** and **Stroke buttons** and the **Swatches panel,**
   change the **fill** colour to *none* and the **stroke** to *black.* Drag
   with the **Rectangle Tool** so you surround all the letters.

5. Change to the **Direct Selection Tool** and click on an
   empty part of the page to de-select the rectangle.

6. Click carefully on the anchor point on the rectangle's bottom
   left to select it. Press the **up arrow key** (on your keyboard) a
   few times to make the left side of the rectangle shorter.

7. Select the rectangle's upper left anchor point and
   bring it down with the **down arrow key.**

8. Using the **Selection Tool,** click on the edge of the rectangle* to select
   it. Hold down the **shift key** and click on the text to select that as well.

9. From the **Object menu** choose *Envelope Distort>Make
   from Top Object* to change the text to match the shape of
   the distorted rectangle. You can adjust the rectangle's shape
   or retype the text until you get the result you want.

* As the rectangle has no fill, if you click on the fill you won't select it.

AIRSHIP-27

1.

Object   Type   Select   Effect

Create Clipping Mask
Create Trim Marks
Flatten Transparency...

Slice   ▶

Path   ▶
Shape   ▶
Pattern   ▶
Blend   ▶
Envelope Distort   ▶   Make with Warp...   ⌥⇧⌘W
Perspective   ▶   Make with Mesh...   ⌥⌘M
Live Paint   ▶   Make with Top Object   ⌥⌘C
Image Trace   ▶   Release
Text Wrap   ▶
Sketch and Line Art   ▶   Envelope Options...

Clipping Mask   ▶   Expand
Compound Path   ▶

2.

T   /
☆   ▦ Rectangle Tool   (M)
       ◻ Rounded Rectangle Tool
       ⬭ Ellipse Tool   (L)
       ⬠ Polygon Tool

3.

AIRSHIP-27

4.

5.

AIRSHIP-27

6.

AIRSHIP-27

7.

Object   Type   Select   Effect

Create Trim Marks
Flatten Transparency...

Slice   ▶

Path   ▶
Shape   ▶
Pattern   ▶
Blend   ▶
Envelope Distort   ▶   Make with Warp...   ⌥⇧⌘W
Perspective   ▶   Make with Mesh...   ⌥⌘M
Live Paint   ▶   **Make with Top Object** ⌥⌘C
Image Trace   ▶   Release
Text Wrap   ▶
Sketch and Line Art   ▶   Envelope Options...

Clipping Mask   ▶   Expand

8.

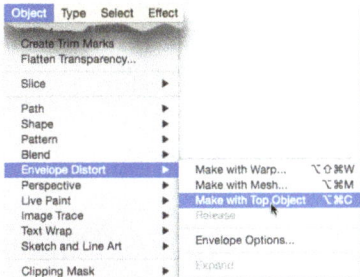

9.

BEBAS NEUE

TO CREATE THIS STENCIL EFFECT YOU'LL MAKE USE OF
BOTH THE FREE TRANSFORM TOOL, AND ANOTHER
OF THE PATHFINDER COMMANDS, DIVIDE.

1. In the same way as you have done before, create appropriately
   sized text with *Bebas Neue* (typed in uppercase). Change
   to the **Selection Tool** and convert the text to outlines.

2. To create the stencil effect, firstly choose the **Rectangle Tool**
   from the **Tools Panel.** Drag with it to create a slim shape that
   will later be used to split the letter into two halves. It doesn't
   matter if the shape extends above or below the letter. If need
   be, change the rectangle's **fill colour** to make it easier to see.

3. To create consistent gaps across all the text, rather than create another
   shape with the Rectangle Tool, change to the **Selection Tool.** Keeping the
   Alt key held down, drag a copy of the shape to overlap the first letter "E".

4. Using the same method, copy the same shape over all the
   remaining letters, leaving aside the "A" and "N" for now.

5. The remaining letters need to be crossed by two shapes,
   which also require rotation. To rotate the shapes, move your
   Selection Tool gradually away from the bottom of the rectangle
   until a curved pair of arrows appears (if you don't see them,
   look in the **View menu** and ensure that *Show Bounding Box*
   is checked). Using *Outline mode* if you need to, drag with
   the arrows to rotate the remaining shapes into place.

6. Select both the text and all the rectangles*. Locate the **Pathfinder
   Panel** (choose **Pathfinder** from the **Window menu** if you can't
   see it) and press the *Divide button* on the panel's bottom left.

7. Using the **Group Selection Tool,** click on an empty part of the
   page to deselect everything. Then click on each rectangle shape
   in turn to select it, and press the *Delete key* to remove it.

* *A good way to do this is to click with your Selection Tool a distance away from everything, then click
  and drag with it over all the shapes. You'll notice a faint rectangle appear which indicates what will
  be selected. Make sure the rectangle either encloses or touches everything you want selected
  (but nothing that you don't), and let your mouse button go to select everything at once.*

BEBAS NEUE. 1.

B. 2. E. 3. BEBAS NEUE. 4.

A A A A A

BEBAS NEUE. 5.

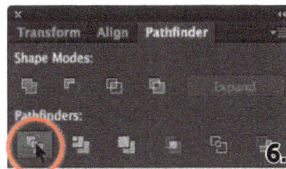

R R R. 7.

BEBAS NEUE

LECO 1976

1. In the same way as you have done before, create appropriately sized text with *Leco 1976* (typed in uppercase). Change to the **Selection Tool** and convert the text to outlines.

2. Still using the **Selection Tool** in combination with the **alt key,** drag a copy of the text diagonally up and left, a little distance away. Shortly you'll create a blend between these two shapes. Before you do that, making sure the text on the upper left is still highlighted, choose *Copy* from the **Edit menu.** You'll make use of this copied text later.

3. Select both pieces of text and choose *Blend>Make* from the **Object menu.** With a blend, Illustrator calculates what an additional object or objects would look like if you blended two others together. In this case as the two original objects are the same, so the additional blended one is too.

4. To create the 3D effect it's simply a matter of creating the blend out of more than one step (as it is by default). To do this, choose *Blend>Blend Options* from the **Object menu.**

5. In the dialogue box that appears, click on *Smooth Color* and choose *Specified Distance* instead. This allows you to specify the exact distance between each step of the blend. To make it appear as one object, use a value of *0.1mm.*

6. Currently you can't really read what the text says, so to create a white copy in front of the blend, firstly choose *Paste in Front* from the **Edit menu.**

7. The text you copied in step 2 now appears in front of the blend. Give this text a fill of *white* (and possibly a black stroke) to finish the logo*.

*   *Whilst the logo is finished, it is made out of a blend that could still be adjusted easily. If you want to change this so that the logo is made out of regular anchor points instead, you could choose **Expand** from the **Object menu.** As there are so many objects created from the expanded blend you could use **Pathfinder's Unite button** to combine them into one shape (be aware that is a complex task that might take some time for Illustrator to do, or even make it crash).*

LECO 1976.

1.

LECO 1976

LECO 1976 **2.**

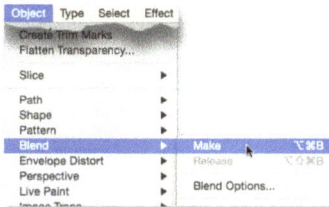

3.

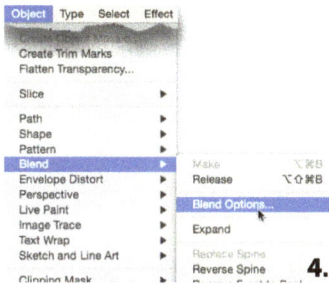

4.

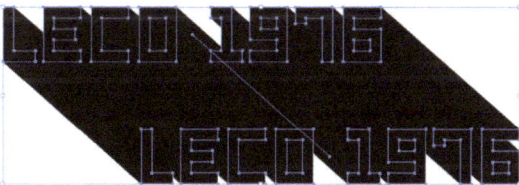

5.

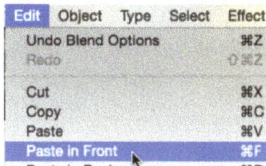

6.

7.

LEARNING CURVE [CS5 or later]

IN THE CREATION OF THIS LOGO YOU'LL LEARN HOW TO USE
THE PENCIL TOOL AND HOW TO MODIFY THE WIDTH OF A
STROKE, A FEATURE INTRODUCED IN ILLUSTRATOR CS5.

1. As you have done before, create *72pt* size text with *Learning Curve Pro.*
   Using the **Selection Tool,** convert the text to outlines then deselect it.

2. Choose the *Pencil Tool** from the **Tools Panel.** You'll use this to
   draw two wavy lines that will flow from both the beginning and end
   of the text. Ensure that the stroke is set to *black,* and the fill to *none.*

3. Position the **Pencil Tool** where you want to start drawing, and
   notice that there is a small "*" next to its tip (it may be an "x" in your
   version) – this means that you're starting to draw a new path.

4. Press the mouse button down and drag to draw either some or all
   of the line. It doesn't matter if you didn't finish the line, or whether
   it needs adjusting, as with the Pencil Tool it's very straightforward
   to change it. If you hover the **Pencil Tool** over the line you've just
   drawn you should notice that the small "x" is no longer there**.
   This indicates that if you drag with it now, you'll either continue
   drawing the line, or redraw an earlier section of the line.

5. Taking as many attempts as you need to, continue drawing and
   redrawing until you've got the lines looking more or less right.

6. If you want to smooth one out without redrawing it, make sure
   it's selected, then change to the *Smooth Tool,* which you'll
   find located beneath the Pencil Tool in the **Tools Panel.** Drag
   with the **Smooth Tool** over any parts that need smoothing.

7. To make your lines blend with the text, in the **Stroke Panel** as well
   as adjusting the stroke **Weight,** choose one of the *Width Profiles* (if
   you have version CS5 or later) that adjusts the stroke's weight along
   its length. If you still want to refine the line further, convert the line
   to outlines using *Path>Outline Stroke* from the **Object menu.** This
   enables you to amend it by either dragging the anchor points with the
   Direct Selection Tool or redrawing parts of it with the **Pencil Tool.**

* *It's also possible to use the Pen Tool to do this, but it's beyond the scope of this book.*

** *If you can see the "x", you're either not hovering over the line, or the line isn't still selected,
so reselect it with the Selection Tool before going back to the Pencil Tool.*

Learning Curve Pro 1.

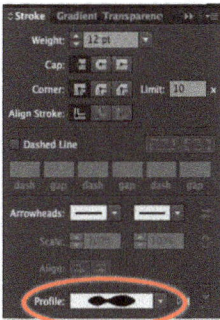

Shaper Tool (Shift-
Pencil Tool
Smooth Tool
Path Eraser Tool
Join Tool

2.

L 3.

Lea 4.

Learning Curve Pro 5.

Learning Curve Pro 6.

Stroke Gradient Transparency

Weight: 1.2 pt
Cap:
Corner: Limit: 10 x
Align Stroke:

Dashed Line

dash gap dash gap dash gap

Arrowheads:

Scale:

Align:

Profile:

Learning Curve Pro 7.

VAL BOLD

IN THE PROCESS OF CREATING THIS LOGO YOU'LL LEARN
HOW TO USE ILLUSTRATOR'S APPEARANCE PANEL TO
COMBINE MULTIPLE STROKES ON THE SAME OBJECT.

1. In the same way as you have done before, create
   72pt size text with *Val Bold.* Change to the **Selection
   Tool** and convert the text to outlines.

2. Make sure the outlined text is all selected, and press the button
   on the right hand side of your screen to reveal the ***Appearance
   Panel.*** Alternatively, choose ***Window>Appearance.***

3. Click on the word *Group* in the panel to apply the appearance
   to the group as opposed to the individual letters. Then
   click the ***Add New Stroke button*** on the bottom left of the
   panel – this adds a virtual stroke on top of the text.

4. Notice that the additional stroke is highlighted in the **Appearance
   Panel,** and that if you click on the word *Stroke,* (or the colour or
   weight) they reveal popup menus. Using these pop-up menus
   adjust the topmost stroke so that it is a *black* stroke of *22pt* weight.

5. Click the **Add New Stroke button** again to add another virtual
   stroke on top of the previous one. Using these pop-up menus
   adjust the topmost stroke so that it is *white* and *20pt* weight.

6. Add a final virtual stroke to your text. Make it *black* and *12pt* weight.

7. To finish* press the **Add New Fill button**
   and give the text a fill of *white.*

8. Now that you can see what effect the different settings have
   on your text, try adjusting different aspects of the different
   strokes. If you have Illustrator CS5 or later, one suggestion
   is to click on the stroke on the bottom, change it to around
   40pt weight and apply either *Width Profile 1* or *2.*

* *As with the LECO logo, if you want to make the effect permanent, you could choose
Expand from the **Object menu.** This applies to the final couple of logos as well.*

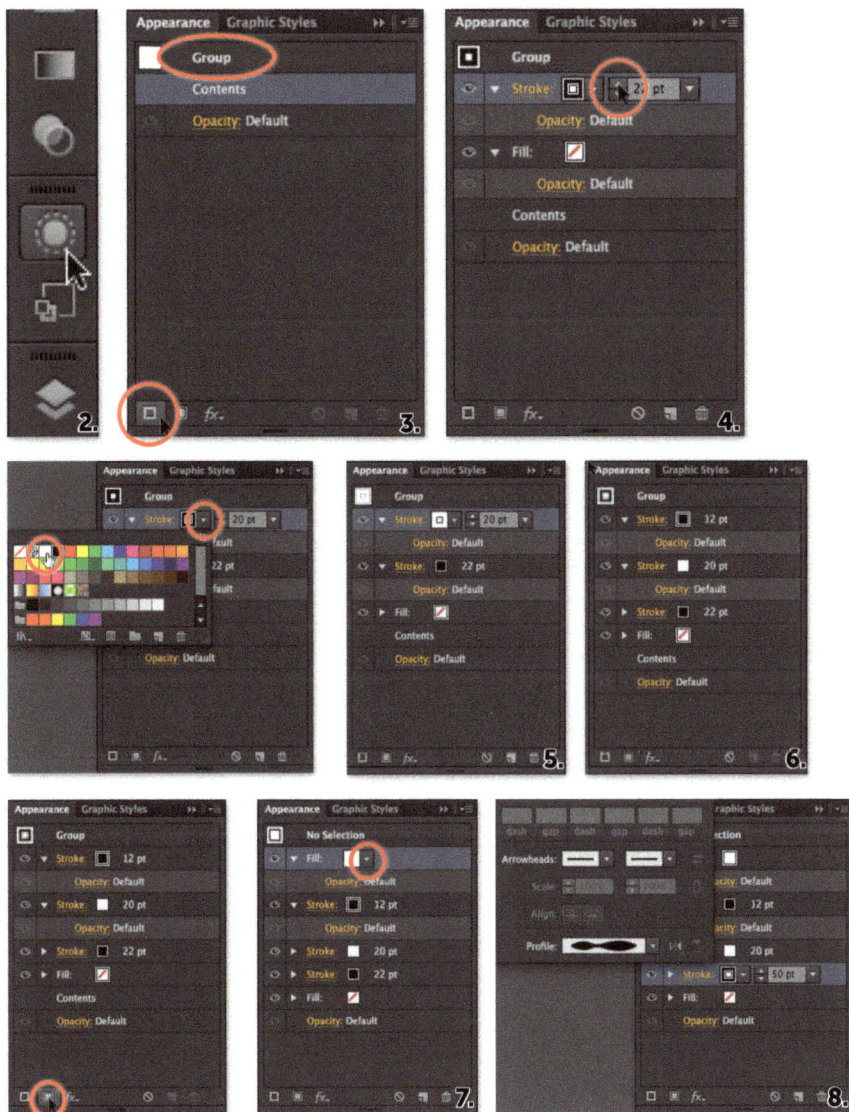

LOBSTER TWO

1. In the same way as you have done before, create *100pt* size text with *Lobster Two Bold.* Change to the **Selection Tool** and convert the text to outlines.

2. Give the text a *light grey* fill and a stroke of *none.*

3. In the **Appearance panel,** press the **Add New Fill button** to give the text an additional fill colour.

4. Change the new fill's colour to *white.*

5. With the white fill still highlighted in the Appearance panel, click on the *FX button* near the panel's bottom left, and choose ***Distort and Transform>Transform.***

6. In the dialogue box that appears, offset the text by *1mm* horizontally and *-1mm* vertically, checking the **Preview** checkbox to see what the result will be before you press **OK.**

7. In the **Appearance Panel,** once again press the **Add New Fill button.** Change the colour of the new fill to *black.* Click on the **FX button** choose **Distort and Transform>Transform** again, and offset this fill by *2mm* horizontally and *-2mm* vertically.

8. This effect will work well on a white background, as the middle band of the text will disappear; if you were going to use the logo on a background other than white, change the colour of the middle band to be that colour instead.

Lobster Two.

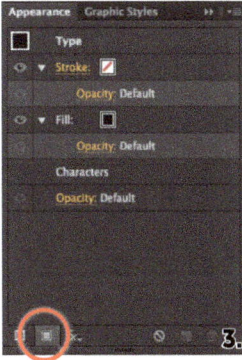

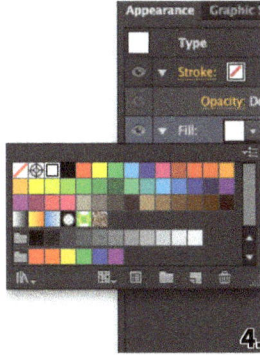

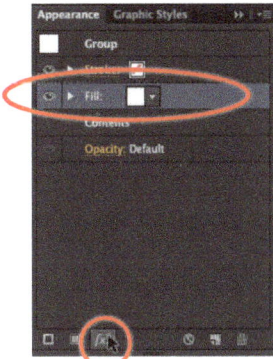

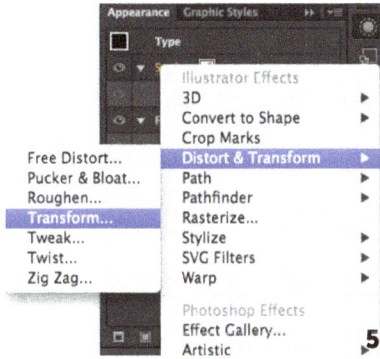

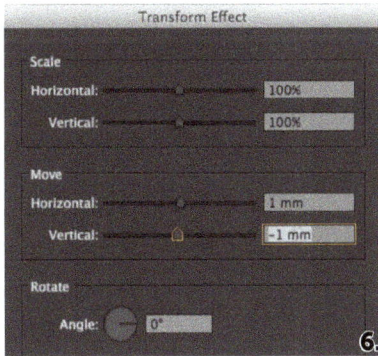

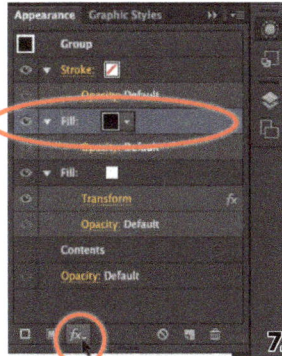

Lobster Two.

7.

OTAMA.EP

IN THE CREATION OF THIS LOGO YOU'LL LEARN HOW
TO CREATE A DIFFERENTLY COLOURED AREA INSIDE
YOUR TEXT, USING THE OFFSET PATH FEATURE.

1. As you have done before, create *72pt* size text with *Otama.ep.*
    Change to the **Selection Tool** and convert the text to outlines.

2. From the **Object menu** choose *Path>Offset Path.* This will
    create a copy of your text that's offset from the original.

3. In the options that have appeared in the dialogue box, a
    positive value creates a copy larger than the original, and
    a negative value makes a smaller offset copy. The different
    join options define what sort of joins will be created in the
    offset path. Choose a *-0.75mm* offset with a *Bevel* join.

4. Whilst your offset text is still selected, choose **Group** from the **Object
    menu.** This groups the offset paths and will make it more easy to
    select it all again, should you need to.* Apply a *white* fill to the text.

5. To finish the logo you'll also fill the inner area with a pattern.
    From the ***Swatches Panel menu*** choose ***Open Swatch
    Library>Patterns>Basic Graphics>Basic Graphics – Lines***.

6. As the default pattern swatches have transparent backgrounds you'll
    need to put the pattern swatch above the white fill in order to see it. To
    do this, go to the **Appearance Panel** and press the **Add New Fill button.**

7. Change the fill colour to one of the lined pattern swatches.

8. In CC or CS6**, press the **Fx button** on the bottom of the **Appearance
    Panel** and choose **Distort & Transform>Transform** from the menu that
    appears. Once in the dialogue box, uncheck the *Transform Objects*
    box and change the scale and rotation of the pattern as desired,
    previewing the result by toggling the *Preview button* on and off.

* *Using the Group Selection Tool it's not only possible to select one object from inside a group, but
   objects within the same sub-group (a group inside a group). Once you've grouped it, the offset text
   has become a sub-group within the larger group. To select it, firstly click on an empty part of the
   page to deselect everything, then double-click on any part of your offset text to select it all.*

** *To scale or rotate the pattern In previous versions of Illustrator you would double-click on either
   the Scale or Rotate tool, uncheck the Transform Objects box and change the scale and rotation
   of the pattern as desired, previewing the result by toggling the Preview button on and off.*

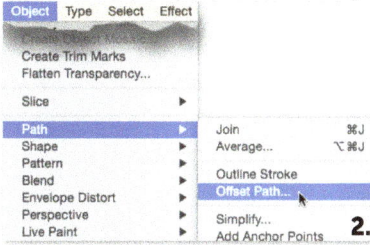

1.

2.

3.

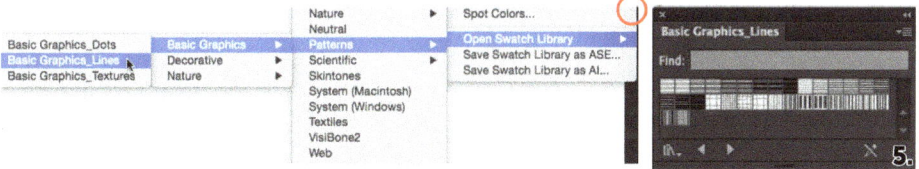

4.

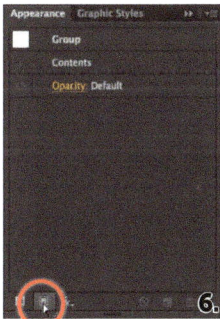

5.

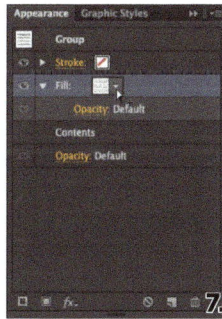

6.

7.

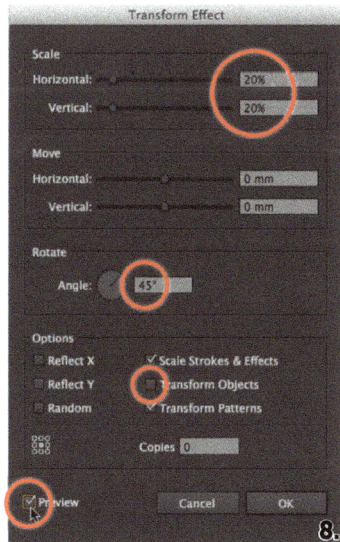

8.

LEAGUE GOTHIC

FOR THE FINAL LOGO YOU'LL CREATE A MUCH MORE COMPLEX BLEND.

1. In the same way as you have done before, create *72pt* size text with *League Gothic* (written in uppercase). Change to the **Selection Tool** and convert the text to outlines.

2. Still using the **Selection Tool,** drag a copy of the text diagonally downwards and to the right, a little distance away. Shortly you'll create a blend between these two shapes. Before you do that, making sure the text on the lower right is still highlighted, choose **Copy** from the **Edit menu.**

3. Select both pieces of text and change their fill colours to *white* and stroke colours to *black.* Make their stroke weights *0.5pt,* and apply a dashed line of *0.5pt* dash and *1pt* gap.

4. With both pieces of text still selected, choose **Blend>Make** from the **Object menu.**

5. Choose **Blend>Blend Options** from the **Object menu,** and change the blend so it has uses a *Specified Distance* value of *0.25pt.*

6. Choose **Paste in Front** from the **Edit menu** to place a copy of the original text in front of the blend. Give it a *white 1pt* stroke to distinguish it from the text behind it.

7. If you want to change the look of the blend, select it with the **Selection Tool** and adjust the blend options, stroke weights or dashed line settings. If you want to change the angle or distance of the blend, firstly deselect everything, then with the **Group Selection Tool** click twice on the text at the back to select just that, and move it up, down, left or right with the appropriate **arrow keys.**

Congratulations on finishing all the logos. I hope you've found the process increasingly intuitive and that you feel inspired to create more. For more creative inspiration, extras and information about our other books, visit **www.designtuitive.com** or follow us at **@designtuitive**

LEAGUE GOTHIC. 1.

LEAGUE GOTHIC. 2.

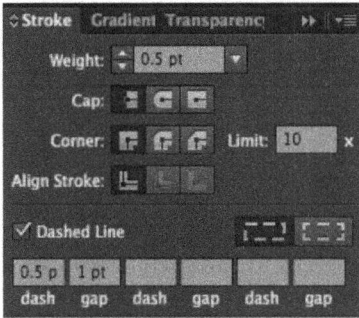

3.

4.

LEAGUE 6.

UPDATES FOR CC 2017 VERSION

Rounded Corners

Since Illustrator CC there has been a new way to give a shape rounded corners. As well as using *Effect>Stylize>Round Corners* (which is featured in the *Rounded Rectangles* chapter) you can now use a feature called *Live Corners.* To use it, simply select a shape such as a rectangle with the **Direct Selection Tool,** and drag the small circle that appears just inside the anchor point. If all the anchor points are selected the whole shape will become rounded, but if an individual anchor points are selected only they will do so. The benefit of this approach is that you can easily experiment with the roundedness of a shape, because you can go back and change it later by using the same approach. The only downside is that unlike the Round Corners Effect, this will physically change the anchor points of your object.

Typekit

Since the previous version of this book the use of *Typekit* has become much more established. If you are a Creative Cloud subscriber you will probably already use TypeKit, as it is bundled free with your CC subscription. It gives you access to thousands of fonts, which you install simply by choosing ***Type>Add Fonts from Typekit*** from within Illustrator. The following fonts used in the *Type* chapter are available on Typekit: *Bebas Neue, League Gothic, Learning Curve, Lobster, and Museo.*

Asset Export

Exporting graphics for online use has become much simpler since Illustrator CC 2017. As well as the approaches mentioned in the *Technical Notes* section, you can simply choose ***Asset Export*** from the **Window Menu.** You simply drag an object into the panel, choose the way you want to export it and press the **Export button.** As well as it being faster than previous approaches there two main benefits of this approach. Firstly, you can export one object that's on an artboard with several others. Secondly, you can export several versions at once – at larger sizes or using different file types.

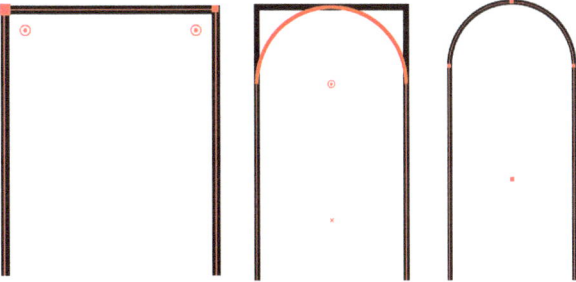

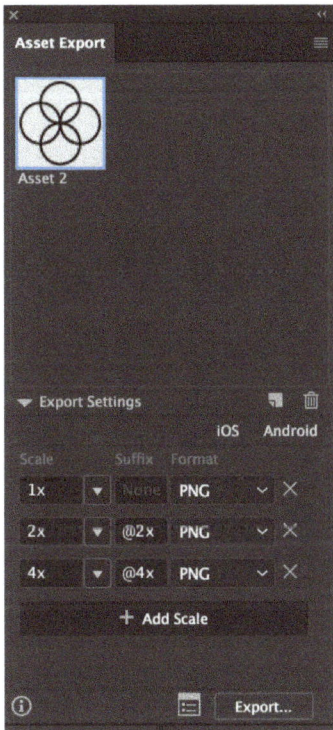

WHAT MAKES A GOOD LOGO?

This book is primarily aimed at giving you the tools and experience you need so you can quickly and easily design logos in Illustrator. But you might also want a little guidance on what makes a good logo. Here are some considerations to bear in mind when creating them.

A logo should work in black and white

No matter what colours you might use in a logo it will likely need to be displayed in either black on white or white on black. Partly for that reason I always create logos in black and white before adding colour.

A logo should work in multiple formats

Try and think more broadly than just a logo that looks good on a computer screen. It might need to be printed using limited colours on a T Shirt, printed large on a billboard or small on a business card. It might need to be used large in a web banner or at a very small size in an app. For that reason I try and mock up logos in a variety of formats when presenting ideas to my clients. If the mock up doesn't work, the actual logo isn't likely to either.

A logo conveys the essence of the brand

Think of a classic logo like the Nike or VW logo. These don't describe what the company does, but nevertheless somehow convey the essence of the brand. When designing a logo for someone I'll spend a lot of time finding out what they are trying to convey, and design the logo accordingly. The choice of typeface and the colours are key to that, as well as any graphic elements.

Less is usually more

Google, Apple, VW, Adidas, BBC. Theirs are all very simple logos. They are not technically difficult to create, but they are great logos partly *because* of that simplicity. I find the hardest part of creating a logo is reducing the available elements down to the absolute essentials.

BRIEF TECHNICAL NOTES

Options with panels

1. Before version CS6, Illustrator's default Tools Panel looked slim like the one on the left (but since CS6 the default is now the double width column, seen on the second left).

2. The way the Tools Panel appears in this book's screenshots is the double width column (seen on the second left). If your tools panel is slim and you want to change it to the double width panel (or vice-versa), press the small pair of white arrows (that look like a Fast-Forward or Rewind button) at the very top of the Tools Panel.

3. Similarly, Illustrator's right-hand panels appear minimal by default like those second from the right.

4. On the far right you'll see there another way of viewing them, used so that you can see a lot more information at once. If you want to do this, press the very similar small pair of white arrows (that look like a Rewind button) at the very top of the panels.

Workspaces

1. If you look in the top right hand corner of your screen you are likely to see the word *Essentials*. This informs you that you are using Illustrator's *Essentials workspace*. A workspace is simply a chosen arrangement of Illustrator's panels – and the default one is the Essentials workspace.

2. If you click on the word *Essentials* you will see it is actually a popup menu – offering you other default workspaces to choose from.

3. Once you've found an arrangement of panels that you like working with, from this popup menu choose ***New Workspace*** and give your workspace a name. Notice that your workspace name is now listed at the top right of the screen, instead of *Essentials*.

4. If later on your panels have changed and you want to get them back to the workspace's default settings, choose ***Reset Essentials*** (or whatever your workspace is called) from the popup menu.

1.

2.

3.

4.

1.

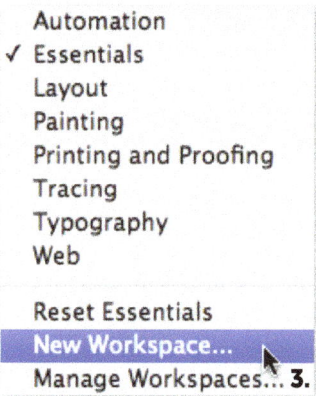

Automation
✓ Essentials
Layout
Painting
Printing and Proofing
Tracing
Typography
Web
Reset Essentials
New Workspace...
Manage Workspaces... **3.**

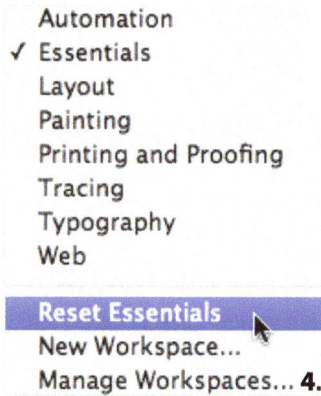

Automation
✓ Essentials
Layout
Painting
Printing and Proofing
Tracing
Typography
Web
Reset Essentials
New Workspace...
Manage Workspaces... **4.**

Illustrator and InDesign

At the risk of oversimplifying a very large subject, Illustrator creates graphics of different types that are generally imported into other programs, most notably InDesign, which is the program most commonly used to create commercially printed documents such as newspapers, magazines and CD covers. In the case of a logo or a map, once created in Illustrator it would be saved in either Illustrator's native .*ai* format, or as an .*eps* file. From InDesign, you'd use the **Place** command from the **File menu** to import the .ai or .eps file. But that's not to say that you'd always look to import your work into InDesign – for many types of work (fashion and packaging are two examples), the Illustrator file is all that's generally used.

Bitmap graphics

If you look at a photograph, whether on screen or printed out, in reality it is simply a large number of equally sized squares, known as *pixels.* At the moment a digital camera takes a photo or a scanner scans a picture, it converts the image before it into pixels. It is because each of these pixels can have their own unique colour that they can be used to represent anything, so long as the pixels themselves are small enough. Photoshop works with images that are created from pixels, which are generically known as *Bitmap* graphics. The bitmap file formats you'll most likely see that are .*jpg* and .*tiff* files.

Vector graphics

Illustrator works with images that are created from *anchor points,* known generically as *vector* graphics. These anchor points define *paths* that can have a fill or a stroke on them, or both. Vector images are much more simplistic than bitmap graphics, but are perfect for the sort of things that have clean, clearly defined areas of colour, such as logos, graphs and maps.

File sizes and quality

In vector graphics the anchor points that make up each shape are defined mathematically. This means that if you make an Illustrator file bigger, behind the scenes the numbers are simply recalculated, and the object is created with no loss in quality. For that reason you can create a logo at a small size and not worry if it is enlarged later. This is different from a bitmap, because each pixel within a bitmap has a physical size. If these types of images are enlarged then each pixel gets larger, making them more visible and potentially reducing the quality of the image.

The size of your document and graphic

If you create a small logo in an A4 sized Illustrator document, when you place that logo into InDesign only the elements that you've drawn will be imported. This is because InDesign can look at the contents of the Illustrator document and only bring in the areas defined by the anchor points. So if you know that you'll be bringing your vector logo, graph, or map into InDesign, in one sense it doesn't matter what size you create them in Illustrator, or in what sized document. However if you are planning to keep your work in Illustrator then it would make sense to make both the document size and the size of your graphic the size you finally want them to be.

Colour — CMYK

The majority of commercially printed work is printed using one of two processes. The first is called *four colour process* (alternatively called *four colour, CMYK, full colour, process colour*). The second is called *spot colour.*

Four colour process works by printing the four process colours, Cyan, Magenta, Yellow and blacK (hence CMYK) in a close arrangement of tiny dots in combinations that can simulate millions of different colours. If you look on the spine of a newspaper you'll probably see the letters CMYK, or possibly little squares or circles printed in those colours. As a general guide, anything you produce that has a colour photograph on it will be produced in Four Colour Process.

Colour — Spot colour

If you look at a document like a letterhead or a business card you'll likely see that it's printed simply using one, two or three colours only. In these instances the print process is more simple: rather than combining the four process inks on the four colour printing press to produce the required colours, pre-mixed inks of the desired colour are bought in and printed on a one, two or three colour printing press. These are known as *spot colours,* or sometimes *specials.* These are perfect for jobs such as business cards where only one, two or three colours are required. If you are designing logos commercially, you will want to provide your client with 2 versions of the same logo: one that is made up of CMYK colours, suitable for using in a magazine, and one that is made of spot colours, suitable for using on a letterhead.

Colour — Pantone colours

The colours you see on screen will not exactly resemble those of your printed document. There are many reasons for this, but the main one is that what you see on a screen is formed by light being "fired" at your eye; whereas what you see in print is formed by light that's reflected from your document to your eye. For that reason alone (and there are many other reasons besides), what you see in print will not appear exactly as it does on the screen.

This can be a problem when choosing colours to use in your work. If you really want to know what a colour will look like when it's printed, you would be advised to look at a *Pantone Book.* Pantone books consist of thousands of *printed* colours, so you can see what they'll look like on paper. There are different books available for different types of print work: inks can be printed in process or spot colour (called *solid* by Pantone) and printed on *coated* (glossy) paper or *uncoated* paper. So, for example, if you wanted to see what your logo's colour should look like when printed in a glossy magazine, you'd look at the *Pantone Process Coated* book. Or if you wanted to see what your logo's colour should look like on your company letterhead you'd look at the *Pantone Solid Uncoated* book.

A particularly useful book for designers is the *Color Bridge* Pantone book, as it shows each colour printed as both a spot and process colour so you can choose one that works well however it is printed. For more about Pantone colours, visit **www.pantone.com**

If you've found colours in a Pantone book that you want to use, make a note of their numbers and you can then use them in Illustrator:

1. Within Illustrator, click on the *Panel menu* on the top right corner of the **Swatches Panel.**

2. From the *Swatches Panel menu* choose *Open Swatch Library>Colour books.* Choose the appropriate book and it will appear as a panel.

3. From the panel's popup menu choose either *Small list view* or *Large list view.* Scroll through the list to find the numbers you want, and then drag them into your **Swatches Panel.** If they are spot colours (from a Pantone *solid* book) they will have a small spot on the bottom-right of the swatch.

Colour – RGB

If what you're producing is destined for the screen, you'll want to use *RGB* colour, a mixture of Red, Green and Blue light used by TVs, monitors, phones and other screens to create colour. When you create a new document, if you choose anything other than *Print* from the *Profile popup menu,* colour will be created using RGB values instead of CMYK ones. **148–149**

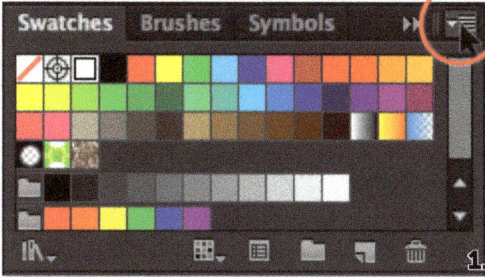

1.

New Swatch...
New Color Group...
Duplicate Swatch
Merge Swatches
Delete Swatch
Ungroup Color Group

Select All Unused
Add Used Colors

Sort by Name
Sort by Kind
Show Find Field

Small Thumbnail View
✓ Medium Thumbnail View
Large Thumbnail View
Small List View
Large List View

Swatch Options...
Spot Colors...

ANPA Color	Art History ▶	**Open Swatch Library ▶**
DIC Color Guide	Celebration	Save Swatch Library as ASE...
FOCOLTONE	**Color Books ▶**	Save Swatch Library as AI...
HKS E Process	Color Properties ▶	
HKS E	Corporate	
HKS K Process	Default Swatches ▶	
HKS K	Earthtone	
HKS N Process	Foods ▶	
HKS N	Gradients ▶	
HKS Z Process	Kids Stuff	
HKS Z	Metal	
PANTONE+ CMYK Coated	Nature ▶	
PANTONE+ CMYK Uncoated	Neutral	
PANTONE+ Color Bridge Coated	Patterns ▶	
PANTONE+ Color Bridge Uncoated	Scientific ▶	
PANTONE+ Metallic Coated	Skintones	
PANTONE+ Pastels & Neons Coated	System (Macintosh)	
PANTONE+ Pastels & Neons Uncoated	System (Windows)	
PANTONE+ Premium Metallics Coated	Textiles	
PANTONE+ Solid Coated	VisiBone2	
PANTONE+ Solid Uncoated	Web	
TOYO 94 COLOR FINDER	User Defined ▶	
TOYO COLOR FINDER	Other Library...	

2.

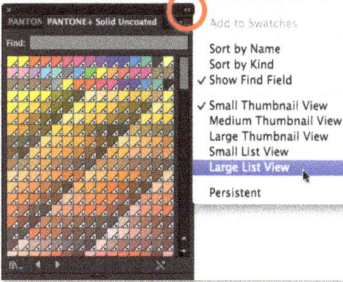

Add to Swatches

Sort by Name
Sort by Kind
✓ Show Find Field

✓ Small Thumbnail View
Medium Thumbnail View
Large Thumbnail View
Small List View
Large List View

Persistent

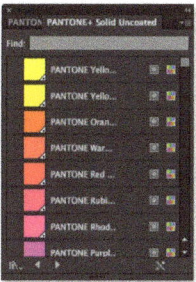

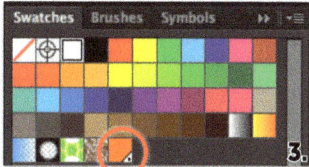

3.

Graphics for the web

In the same way that Illustrator can create graphics that can be imported into InDesign for printed documents, it can also create graphics that can be placed on web pages.

1. When you create a new document, choose *Web* from the options shown. This changes the colour mode you'll work in to *RGB,* changes the measurement system to *Pixels* and offers you commonly used web page sizes, like *1920 x 1080 pixels.*

2. The file formats we've already discussed (the *.ai* and the *.eps*) are *vector* file formats used widely in print. But the formats most widely used on websites are the *bitmap* file formats *.png, jpg,* and *.gif.* Most designers and developers have settled on .png as the best format to use. One way to turn your (vector) Illustrator graphic into a .png is to choose **Export>Export for Screens*** from the **File menu.**

3. Since Illustrator CC 2017 the **Asset Export panel** has become the quickest way to export a graphic for on screen use. You may have already read about this in the *Updates for CC 2017* section of this book.

4. An alternative approach to take if you're looking to create a graphic of a specific size (eg 30 x 30 pixels) is to create a page of that exact size and align your graphic to the edges of the document. If you know you are going to save the file as a .png, another option is to simply choose **Export>Export As** from the **File menu** to save a *.png* version of your file. A dialogue box appears giving you some quick, useful options.

Graphics for mobile devices, video and film

In the same way that Illustrator offers you the appropriate colour mode, page sizes and measurement systems when creating graphics for print and web, it gives you similarly useful options if you choose the *Mobile* or *Film and Video* document profiles when creating a new document. Diagram 5 shows some of the sizes available in Illustrator CC 2017's *Mobile* document profile.

*   *This largely replaced the previous **File>Save for Web** (now also in the Export sub menu).*

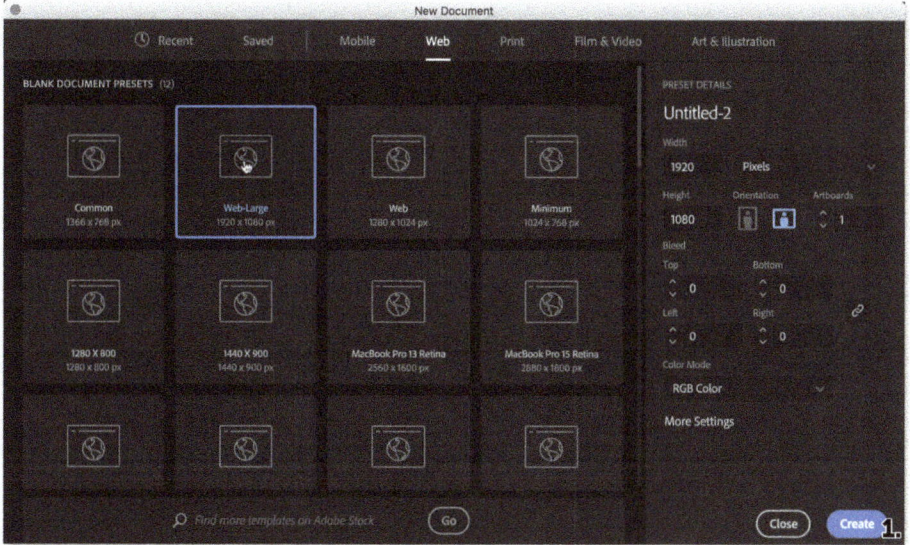

1.

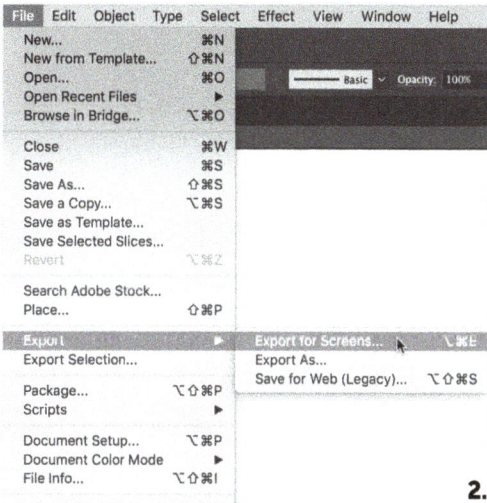

2.

5.

Three options when creating these logos

There are three distinct approaches you could take when creating the logos in this book. If you've not yet created them, take a moment to decide which of them you'll use.

1. The first approach is to create all the logos in one large document. The advantage of this is that everything is kept together in one place. However one disadvantage is that as these logos are quite small (in comparison with the size of the page), you need to be confident zooming in, out and around the page. Another disadvantage is that later on if you wanted to place any of the logos into InDesign, you'd probably need to copy and paste each logo into its own file. To use this approach, choose **New** from the **File menu** at the top left of your screen. For the purposes of this book, my assumption is that you want to create logos that will be printed – so in the dialogue box that appears, choose *Print* from the *New Document Profile popup menu* and press the **OK button.**

2. The second approach is to create every logo in a separate document. If you're going to do that, you'd probably want to make the size of your document a bit smaller so you don't need to zoom in so much. To use this approach, create a new document as described above, then change the document's *Width* and *Height* values to somewhere around *50mm*.

3. The third approach you could take is to use multiple *artboards* (introduced in Illustrator CS4) whereby you can have several "pages" of the same size next to each other in the same document. There are several advantages to this approach: firstly, everything is kept together in one document; secondly, as every logo is created on its own "page" you can make use of the **Command + 0** shortcut to quickly fit that page to the screen (and **Command + Alt + 0** to show all the pages at once). However a disadvantage is that having all the logos appearing next to each other can actually make it more difficult to align objects, as the Smart Guides are likely to try and align the logo you're currently working on with something else on one of the other artboards. To use this approach, create a new document as described before, but then change the number of *Artboards* to *12* and change the *Width* and *Height* values to somewhere around *50mm*.

If you're new to Illustrator I'd recommend creating everything inside one A4 document, and then revisiting the exercises using multiple artboards at a later date.

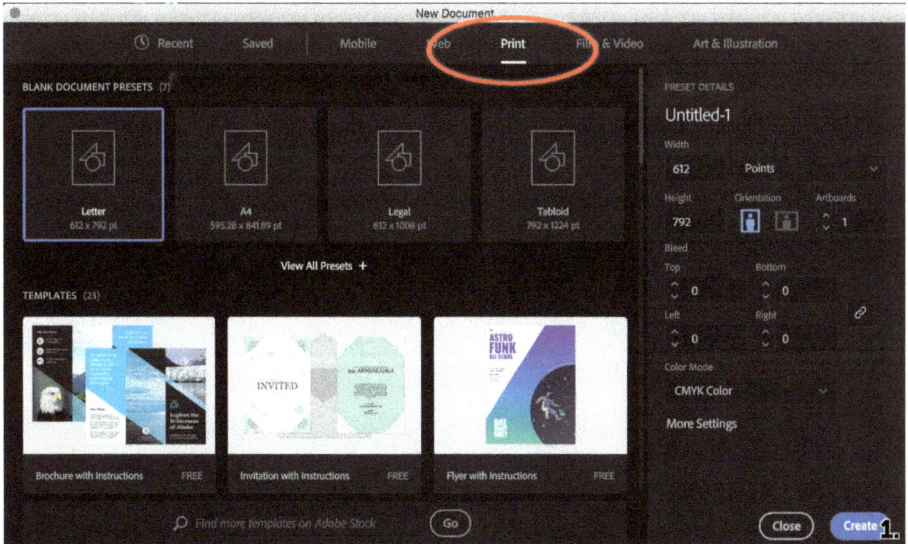

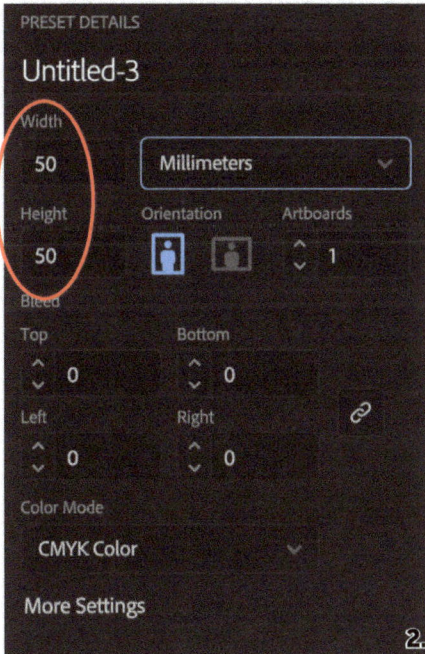

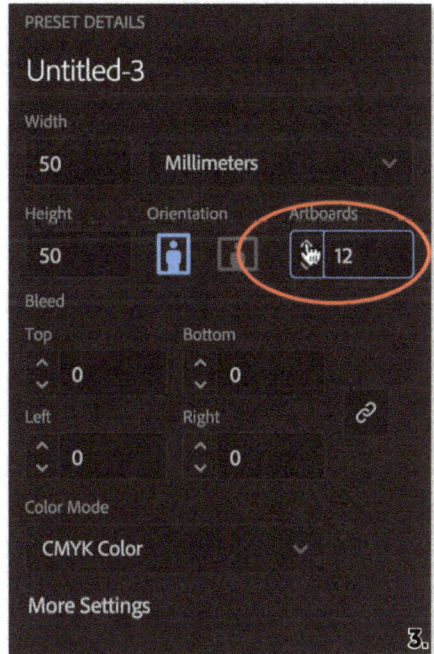

More about multiple Artboards

1. When you are working with multiple artboards notice the subtly darker edge of the artboard you are currently working with, as shown in diagram 1. If you use the **Command + 0** shortcut, this is the artboard you will zoom into.

2. To align an object to an artboard firstly select it, then locate the align popup menu towards the top right of your screen, and from it choose **Align to Artboard.** This is the default setting, and means that when you press the align buttons to the right, the object you have selected will move to align itself to the artboard (instead of other objects you might have selected). Press the **Horizontal Align Center** and **Vertical Align Center** buttons to align your object to the middle of the artboard.

3. If you have an object aligned on one artboard that you would also like on another artboard, select it, and choose **Copy** from the **Edit menu.** Then with your **Selection Tool** click on the artboard you'd like to copy it to (its edge should darken slightly to indicate it's the active artboard) and choose **Paste in Place** from the **Edit menu.**

4. If you wanted to copy the same object onto all the artboards, you'd repeat the previous process, but choose **Paste on All Artboards** from the **Edit menu** instead of **Paste in Place** (but be aware it will paste a copy onto *all* the artboards, even ones that already have things on them – so watch out for duplicate copies).

5. Supposing you have created several different versions of a logo, each on a different artboard, and now you'd like to save a copy of just one or two of them as a pdf to show your colleague or client. First you'll need to know the names of the artboards that your logos are on. To do that, choose the **Artboard Tool** from the **Tools Panel.**

6. You're now in *artboard editing mode*: you can see each of the artboards and their names (it's also possible to resize, reorder, create and delete artboards here). Make a note of the artboard(s) you want to export. Change to the **Selection Tool** to leave artboard editing mode.

7. From the **File menu** choose **Save a Copy.** In the dialogue box that appears, choose *Adobe PDF* format and type the number of the artboard you which to save. If you want to save several, separate contiguous numbers (eg 2-5) with a dash, or otherwise with a comma (eg 3,7).

1.

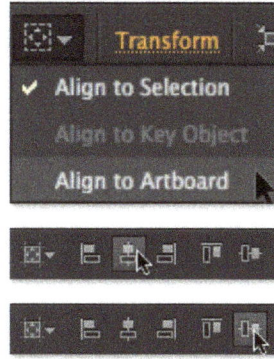
2.

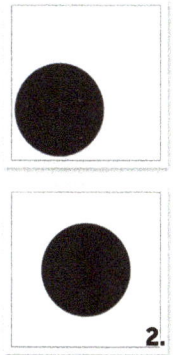
3.

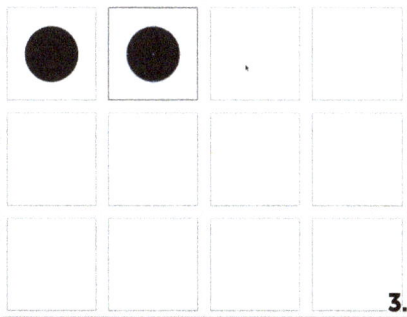
4.

5.

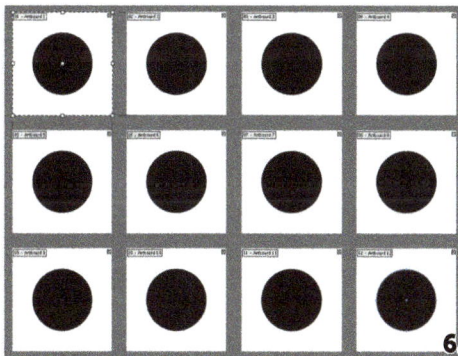
6.

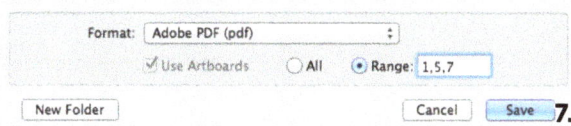
7.

ABOUT DESIGNTUITIVE

Designtuitive is a small independent publisher.
We make books and videos to help you get the most out of
creating software like InDesign, Illustrator and Photoshop.
Designtuitive.com
@designtuitive

ABOUT THE AUTHOR

Peter Bone has worked in graphic design for 25 years. During that time he
has taught thousands of people to use Quark Xpress, Indesign, Illustrator
and Photoshop – at every level from complete beginners through to
experts in their field. He has taught designers, marketers, creative directors,
writers, editors, illustrators, fashion designers and photographers for
organisations as varied as The BBC, The British Museum, Condé Nast, The
Designers Guild, Disney, Greenpeace, The Guardian, Ralph Lauren, Paul
Smith, Price Waterhouse Coopers and the United Nations.
peterbone.com
*@PeterBone_*